MW01004223

THE ORVIS POCKET GUIDE TO FLY FISHING FOR
Striped Bass and Bluefish

Books by Lou Tabory

Stripers on the Fly
Inshore Fly Fishing
*Lou Tabory's Guide to Saltwater Baits and Their
 Imitations*

THE ORVIS POCKET GUIDE TO FLY FISHING FOR
Striped Bass and Bluefish

LOU TABORY

Illustrations by Rod Walinchus

The Lyons Press

Copyright © 2001 by Lou Tabory
Illustrations copyright © Rod Walinchus

10 9 8 7 6 5 4 3 2 1

Printed in China

Library of Congress Cataloging-in-Publication Data
Tabory, Lou.
    The Orvis pocket guide to fly fishing for striped bass and bluefish /
    Lou Tabory.
      p. cm.
    ISBN 1-58574-076-4
     1. Striped bass fishing. 2. Bluefishing. 3. Saltwater fly fishing.
I. Title: Fly fishing for striped bass and bluefish. II. Title.

  SH691.S7 T33 2001
  799.1'7732—dc21

                                     00-48665

CONTENTS

ACKNOWLEDGMENTS

To my wife, Barb, for all her help and patience.
To my favorite editors, Nick Lyons and
Angus Cameron.
To Perk and Dave Perkins, Randy Carlson,
Tom Rosenbauer, and Paul Fersen for
keeping me employed.
For all my fishing friends—you know who you are—
thanks for all your help and the fun times together.

FOREWORD

Mark Twain once said, "I didn't have time to write you a short letter so I wrote you a long one," referring to the fact that it's harder work to say the same thing in fewer words. Lou Tabory has done an amazing job of getting all the essential information a striper or bluefish fly rodder needs in a book that will fit in your shirt pocket. It's all here: special casting hints, picking the right equipment, choosing flies, finding fish, retrieving flies, and playing and landing stripers and blues. You'll learn how to fish everything from rocky cliffs to shallow flats with water the transparency of a mountain spring. And how many fishing books give you advice on "when to move and when to hang tough"?

Fly fishing along the East Coast is nothing new; colonial anglers caught stripers on salmon flies, and flies tied especially to catch stripers were common by the first half of the 20th century. After World War II, however, striper fishing with flies was overshadowed by the advent of spinning rods and war-surplus Jeeps that were turned into beach buggies. In the past 10 years, however, fly fishing for stripers and blues has turned into a craze, with passions and tackle and fly development on an unprecedented level. Only 20 years ago, when there was exactly one saltwater fly rod guide on the East Coast, people stared at us and laughed at our fly rods on Lobsterville Beach, which is now one of the most famous fly-rod striper places in the world. I would drive from Vermont to Connecticut and Martha's Vineyard for long sleepless weekends of striper fishing with some of the young hotshots who were just beginning to discover the fishery. None of us had ever fished with Lou Tabory, but he was our God. He'd been at it for years before us, and once in a while a figure would appear out of the dawn mist at Compo Beach in Westport with a shy smile and warm greeting. It was Lou, and of course he'd taken some big fish while we were taking a short nap.

I'd also see Lou at sports shows, where he put on fly-casting demonstrations. His silky casting and easy, humble, soft-spoken manner was in sharp contrast to many of the barkers putting on demonstrations. A couple of us from Orvis talked Lou into consulting for us, because we felt his talents were perfectly suited for what our company was doing. Lou soon began teaching fly fishing and fly casting full time. There is no one from the East Coast saltwater fishery who combines Lou's knowledge of baitfish (he's written another book called *Lou Tabory's Guide to Saltwater Baits and Their Imitations*), tackle (he has been a tackle consultant for years), beaches (he used to be a surfer), casting, and just great tips that could only come from someone who's spent decades studying salt water.

This is the book you want for your first introduction to stripers and bluefish, or if you only want to carry one book on your fishing trips. You can do no better than heed Lou Tabory's solid advice.

—*Tom Rosenbauer*

INTRODUCTION

The biggest misconception about saltwater fly fishing is that you need to make a long cast. One of the first things I tell my students when I'm teaching a fly-fishing clinic is: "If you can cast 40 feet, you can catch fish in the sea." A second misconception is that you need to travel to some exotic destination to find first-rate saltwater fly fishing. The fact is that there's quality fly fishing for stripers and bluefish just a short drive from many of the cities along the eastern seaboard.

Catching striped bass and bluefish on fly tackle isn't difficult, but it can be overwhelming, because the sea is so big. At first glance, its size fills most anglers with awe. The key, then, is selecting the water that's right for you, water that you can fish easily. Certain water types require different skill levels. For the beginner, this means staying away from conditions that are too difficult. A beginning golfer doesn't play his first round at Augusta; a novice fly rodder shouldn't take on 30-knot winds, or attempt to fish in 6-foot waves along an ocean beach.

Fly fishing should be fun and relaxing. Time on the water is something you should look forward to: a positive, enjoyable experience where you continually learn to become a better angler. This book is meant to guide you through the early pitfalls that trip up many beginners, and to become a constant source of information as you develop into a better angler. If you're starting a new sport, or a beginner in a different type of fishing, the important thing is to learn the basics first. I've become a successful fly rodder because I keep learning new techniques, but I also continue to employ the basics. You'll always use the basic techniques: They work.

After mastering fundamentals, you'll find that more difficult water types and rougher water conditions will be less of a mystery. Each new experience, each different water type will help make you a better angler. Saltwater fly fishing for stripers and bluefish is relatively new; anglers with 10 years of experience are "old salts." Even if you're a beginning fly rodder, you're not far behind.

Study the casting techniques and fishing strategies in this book, and you'll learn the fundamentals of fishing for stripers and bluefish from Maine to the Carolinas. The basic water types exist from the outer beaches of North Carolina to the river systems of the Chesapeake, the clear waters around Cape Cod, and the cliffs of Maine. In some locations, you'll find many water types in a single day's fishing. Remember, you'll use the same techniques in different locations if their water conditions and tide sizes are the same. A fish's feeding habits don't change when it swims from state to state.

SETTING UP TACKLE AND GEAR

RODS

The exceptional tackle we have today is a major reason for the recent explosion of saltwater fly fishing. Rods are lighter, stronger, and much easier to cast. Graphite is the best material for saltwater rods; fiberglass and bamboo aren't even close seconds. Pay $200 to $300, and you will own an exceptional casting tool.

There are some major differences between fresh- and saltwater fly equipment, most of them relating to size. Simply, you need bigger tackle when fishing the sea: You need enough line weight to fight wind and cast bigger flies, and you need enough rod power not only to cast, but also to land fish.

Rods are made to match lines of different weights, beginning at No. 1 and running up to No. 15. Most saltwater anglers use rods ranging from 6- to 12-weight, the most popular rod size for stripers and bluefish being a 9-foot 9-weight. The 9-weight is ideal for many water types and will handle all but the most demanding locations. You must look at your home waters, along with the other water types you plan to fish, before deciding what size tackle to buy. If you intend to fish with tiny flies inside small estuaries for small fish, or will fish mostly shallow flats and sheltered beaches, a 7- or 8-weight rod will work fairly well.

Other than rod action, look for two good-sized stripping guides, a comfortable handle, and a good fighting butt.

But if you want to cover a variety of waters, get a heavier rod so you'll have more options. If you'd like to fish open surf, rocky cliffs, or big rips—or you plan to use heavy sinking lines and fish with big flies— you'll need a 9- or even a 10-weight rod.

If I could use only one fly rod, it would be a nine-foot 10-weight. That's my workhorse. I like to fish bigger waters, bigger flies, and heavier conditions without struggling; in fact, I prefer to be overgunned. I seldom fish with anything smaller than a 9-weight. To make your own choice, consult your local tackle dealer, talk with fly-fishing friends, then try casting several different rod sizes.

Another factor to consider is rod action; be sure to try different actions to see which one fits your casting style. Rod actions range from full flex to tip flex. Most anglers prefer midflex rods, 6.5 to 8.0 flex. The Orvis Company has developed a system that classifies each rod action; 6.5 to 8.0 are the flex rates I prefer too. These work better if you're casting sinking lines or fishing big flies. A midflex rod is also more forgiving when you're fishing in low light; you can feel the line better. It's less tiring when you cast for long periods, and is the best choice for the beginning caster. For sight casting, or fishing small flies with a floating line, many experienced anglers prefer a tip-flex action, around 9.5 flex. It gives more speed when casting to sighted fish. And if you overload a tip-flex fly rod by one line size—putting a No. 10 fly line on a 9-weight rod, for instance—it approximates a midflex rod. If you choose a 9-weight tip-flex rod, you can sight cast with a floating line and then use a No. 10 intermediate line to slow the rod for night fishing and casting bigger flies.

REELS

Fly reels come in a vast range of types and prices. The reels in the $100 to $200 range work well; if you don't have a big budget and want a finely crafted reel, there are many to choose from. If you can consider more expensive reels, look for one with a large arbor. Large-arbor reels retrieve line more quickly when you're fighting a fish, especially if it runs back toward you. The fly line also has fewer coils when you take it off the reel because of the spool's larger diameter.

Reels come in all types and price ranges. Pick the best one you can afford, with interchangeable spools.

There are now some good large-arbor reels in the $200 to $300 range.

A good saltwater fly reel should have a sound drag, an exposed-spool rim for palming (applying drag with your hand), and a counterweighted spool. It should be durable, have noncorrosive parts, and hold plenty of backing. Most modern saltwater reels meet all these requirements and, with minimal maintenance, will give you good service for many years.

I like reels whose spools are quickly changeable when I'm switching fly-line types. If you must disassemble a reel to change spools, you might lose parts or not reassemble the reel properly. Juggling reel parts on

Fly reels with easy replaceable spools make line changing simple. Large arbor reels (right) also let you retrieve line more quickly.

a sandy beach at night, or in a bouncy boat, or when wading in deep water, is an invitation to disaster.

There are two basic reel designs: direct drive and antireverse. A direct-drive reel has the handle attached to the spool, and spins when a fish runs. The handle on an antireverse reel doesn't spin and won't crack the fingers on your reeling hand when a fish runs.

Direct-drive reels, on the other hand, provide more positive reeling power, and better control at night because you take in line with each rotation of the reel's handle. With an antireverse, the clutch can slip if you're reeling against a heavy fish; you never really know if you're gaining line. The direct drive is the more popular reel, and the choice of the experienced angler.

BACKING

A common mistake that anglers make is buying a reel that doesn't hold enough backing. The backing—Dacron, Micron, or gel-spun poly—goes onto the spool first; the fly line is then knotted to the backing. Unlike most freshwater fishing situations, in salt water you'll hook fish that make long runs, often longer than 50 yards. I recommend 150 yards of backing for the boat angler and 200 yards for the surf angler. You may never need more than 100 yards, but you'll be glad for the extra yardage the day a big fish tries to clean your spool. I use either 30-pound Dacron or 50-pound gel-spun poly. Dacron is the most popular backing because it's less expensive and has been used by fly rodders for

I like heavier backing, 30-pound Dacron or 50-pound gel-spun poly.

years; 50-pound poly is smaller in diameter, allowing you to put more backing on a smaller reel, and is more durable. I don't recommend 35-pound poly for a novice, because its thin diameter can cause severe cuts if the backing wraps around you or if you even touch it while a fish is running. One angler told me a horror story about loose line winding around his bare leg as a big fish ran out his backing. The thin line cut deeply into his thigh, causing a serious wound that required many stitches. Twenty-pound Dacron is too light for many fishing situations, and it isn't as durable. If you use a 20-pound tippet with 20-pound backing, the knot between the fly line and backing might break before the tippet does. Fly lines are expensive: Use heavier backing.

A fly reel should convert easily from right- to left-hand wind. I can reel with both hands, but I primarily use my left hand to reel, holding the rod with my casting hand. I don't change hands when fighting a fish. There is no "correct" hand for reeling. Use the one that lets you reel efficiently and comfortably. Don't let anyone bully you into reeling with the wrong hand because they claim it's the best way.

Fly Line

The weight-forward fly line is the best choice for most saltwater fly fishing. The intermediate fly line, however, is the most effective and versatile line for stripers and blues. This is a slow-sinking fly line that's either colored or clear. It casts better than a floater, it

Choose the right fly line. Although the intermediate line is more versatile, the clear sinking tip might be better for the beginner.

settles slowly while avoiding the effects of wind, and it gets the fly down deep enough without causing the casting problems of a fast-sinking line. (Fast-sinking lines are heavy to cast and hard to lift from the water.) I use it for perhaps 60 percent of my fishing. In fact, the intermediate should be the first fishing-line choice for most anglers.

I use a floating line for special fishing situations, like when there's a worm hatch and I'm sight casting in very shallow water. But for most of my sight fishing, for fishing poppers, and for fishing shallow shorelines at night, I use a clear-tipped fly line. This line has a clear, 10-foot intermediate tip spliced to a floating fly line. The 10-foot clear section allows me to fish a shorter leader—3 to 4 feet long—which turns over much better than a longer leader, especially when I'm casting into the wind or I'm using big flies and poppers. It's a very useful line, far more versatile than the floating kind. The clear tipped is the ideal choice for anglers who sight cast or fish shallow sheltered beaches at night.

Learning to use a fast-sinking line will take time, particularly for the beginner. These lines are very useful, however, especially in fast-flowing rips or rolling surf. They handle big flies well and will cut through tough winds. Fast-sinking lines like the Depth Charge are a better choice for most anglers. Shooting heads do work well, but they are more difficult to cast and handle. A Depth Charge has a 30-foot head of fast-sinking line, with 70 feet of intermediate running line. They cast like shooting heads and handle like weight forwards. Fast-sinking lines work well for some shallow-water applications and for shore fishing in heavy surf, but it takes experience and quick line handling to fish them properly. Learn how to fish fast-sinking lines in deep water before attempting to use them in shallow water.

Let the tackle shop owner or company that sells you your equipment set up your line system, from the reel spool right down to the loop on the end of the fly line.

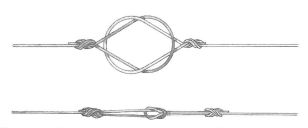

This is the right way to interlock two loops when putting the leader onto the fly line.

Most fly lines have a loop knotted to the end of the line. To this loop, attach a 7½- or 9-foot knotless tapered leader by interlocking the two loops. Just connect the loop on the tapered leader to the loop on the fly line and you're ready to go fishing; no elaborate knotting system here.

KNOTS AND LEADERS

Keep your leader and knotting system simple by using tapered leaders. Enjoy the fishing first, then become a knot fanatic later. You only need several knots—one to tie on the fly, or bite guard, and one to attach additional tippet material—to fish for bass and blues. The improved clinch knot is perhaps the best-known knot for tying on flies; it's very strong with most leader materials maintaining better than 90 percent breaking strength. For tying on tippet material—either adding to the tapered leader as it shortens, or lengthening a full-sized leader if you're sight fishing to spooky fish—use a surgeon's knot. Both these knots are popular and easy to tie.

Which is the better material for a leader, nylon monofilament or fluorocarbon? Nylon has better knot strength and is less expensive, while fluorocarbon is more durable and less visible. What you lose in knot strength with fluorocarbon you gain in total strength, because you can use a heavier tippet. I've used fluorocarbon for three years, with excellent results. Remember to use either one material or the other: Knotting

Keep the leader system simple. A tapered leader, a spool of tippet material, and you are ready to go fishing.

monofilament to fluorocarbon doesn't work, as the knot will slip at a low breaking strength.

Bluefish have sharp cutting teeth, so you should use a wire bite guard to prevent them from biting through the tippet. There are several types of bite guards. One involves unraveling the twisted wire, attaching the fly, then twisting it back to close the locking device. Another good bite guard is a short wire leader with a snap for changing the fly. Both devices are easy to use: Just tie on the bite guard as you would a fly, then change the fly without using a knot. I like the shortest, lightest bite guard I can find.

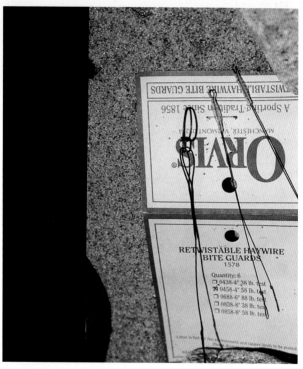

Use a bite guard that is small and light when bluefish are around.

HOW TO TIE A GOOD KNOT

Tying strong knots requires several simple steps. Start by using good, fresh leader materials. Form the knot carefully, wet it with saliva, and pull it slowly so it tightens correctly. Be sure to pull the knot hard enough to test its strength. If the knot is poor, it will break in your hand, not on a fish. Learning to tie a few good knots well is one of the keys to successful fishing.

OTHER GEAR

A stripping basket is a device that holds loose fly line while you're fishing. It makes casting easier, minimizes tangles, and, if you're standing in moving water, keeps loose line from drifting away or wrapping around your feet. Wading anglers would be lost without them, but they also work well in boats. I prefer the hard, rectangular baskets that feature cones on the bottom; these cones keep the line from flopping around in the wind, or from tangling when I'm moving from spot to spot. Learn to use one; it will be one of the most important pieces of fishing equipment you own.

Stripping baskets are very useful, especially when you're wading.

I like boot-foot waders for most shore fishing. They're easy to put on and take off, they're light in weight, and the boot foot is better for walking in the sand than stocking-foot waders and wading boots. The no-sweat models are great for long walks and for warm-weather fishing. If you plan to wade in cold water for extended periods, wear good insulated underwear or neoprene waders.

You need to carry extra tapered leaders, tippet material, flies, pliers, a hook sharpener, sunglasses, a light for night fishing, and a compass if you're wading long distances in big-tide areas. I use a small bag to carry all this gear, but most anglers prefer a chest pack or a

Some basic gear for fly fishing the salt (clockwise, from left): a light to change flies, a stronger light to find your way, pliers, hook sharpener, and compass (in the center).

vest. Choose whatever you like; just remember that the bigger it is, the more junk you'll carry.

Having the right equipment and setting it up properly makes learning to fly fish for stripers and bluefish much easier. If you start out by fighting with poor equipment, it will just take that much longer to enjoy the sport.

2

FLY CASTING

Over the years, I've taught fly casting to many anglers. Those who listened learned quickly. The best beginning caster I ever saw was a young lady named Amy who attended a fly-fishing clinic at Nantucket several years ago. By the second day she was throwing 2-foot-wide loops, making 70-foot casts with power. Meanwhile, several guys in the class were flailing away—as most people do—trying to find their timing.

It's always fun to watch casters like Amy start to shoot line as their technique comes together. I've seen anglers struggle for the better part of two days, then suddenly start shooting line with authority. It's gratifying to watch someone pick up casting quickly, but this isn't usually the case. People have different learning curves; some anglers need more time to learn the techniques of casting. If you start properly, however, and master the fundamentals, fly casting won't be a chore to learn.

Many anglers have the wrong impression about saltwater fly fishing, believing that long casts are a necessity. They lack the confidence to try fishing the sea because they can't make long casts. But if you can throw 40 feet of fly line, you can catch fish. There are many places, particularly at night, when a cast of this distance might even be too long. Learning to cast well makes fishing easier, however, and gives you more opportunities to fish a broader range of water types. Being a better caster also helps you fish in wind, cast bigger flies, and use sinking lines.

My goal in this book is to make your fishing easier by helping you improve your casting techniques. If you're a total beginner, get some help by reading some good books, watching some videos, or, even better, attending a fishing or casting clinic.

GRIPPING THE ROD

Hold out your casting hand, palm up, and lay the rod on it so the handle crosses your palm from the joint of your first finger to the heel of your hand. Grip the rod handle with all four fingers and roll your thumb so it holds the rod comfortably. The thumb should be slightly rolled to the side and not straight up on top of the rod. It must rest on the rod, and not wrap over your fingers. Don't use a stranglehold—just a good firm grip. If you feel any numbness, loosen your grip. Your first few casting sessions should be short, with pauses every five minutes so you can relax your casting hand. I advise my students to switch the rod to the other hand and shake the casting hand.

USING THE WHOLE BODY

To make a good fly cast, employ your whole body, especially your shoulder and arm. Use your wrist only at the end of the cast to stop the rod; your shoulder and arm should do most of the rest of the work, and almost

The proper way to grip the rod. Note thumb is on top of the handle, and slightly rolled off to the right of a right-handed caster. It would be to the left, on a left-handed caster.

all of the cast's setup. Never break your wrist during the cast, as this will cause the cast to fall apart. The wrist does stop the rod at the end of both the back- and forward cast, however, thus adding extra power to the cast. But you should never make the full cast with your wrist, because it will tire easily. Also, this usually causes the rod tip to swing in an arc, which is a major casting fault.

THE BACKCAST

Pinch the line under the first finger of your casting hand during your first several casting sessions, leaving your other hand relaxed at your side. This will focus all your attention onto making the basic casting stroke without adding the complications of the other hand. For a right-handed caster, the rod should begin parallel to the ground, in the 9 o'clock position. Raise the rod slowly from 9 o'clock to 11 o'clock. This is called the pickup; it breaks the grip of the water on the line, and it loads the rod. You must move the line before casting to break the water's grip on the fly line; you won't notice this when you're casting on grass, but once you graduate to water it will be evident.

From the 11 o'clock position, with the rod loaded, sweep the rod back briskly to the 1:30 position, then stop the rod firmly. Perform the pickup and backcast in one continuous motion, and do so with your shoulder, arm, *and* wrist, not just the wrist (think back to the last section). This is called the backcast because it travels behind you and sets up the forward cast. Without a

Beginning the cast with the rod position low is essential.

Raise the rod slowly. This breaks the water's grip on the line and loads the rod for the backcast.

good backcast, your forward cast will never become strong. Remember, the rod tip must travel in a straight line from 11 o'clock to 1:30. If the tip travels in an arc, your loop will be large and have no power.

The line forms a loop as it travels through the air. The key to a good fly cast is a tight loop. To make a tight loop—one that's less than 3 feet wide—the rod tip must travel in a straight line, and the rod must stop cleanly. Making clean, positive stops will add power and line speed to your casts.

WATCHING THE BACKCAST

Watch the rod tip to be sure that it flows through the air on a level plane. Watching the rod tip and the loop is a good way to learn timing. Pay special attention to

When casting, the proper foot position is about a 45-degree angle to the direction of the cast. This stance makes it much easier for the angler to watch his or her backcast.

the loop as it unrolls on the backcast; begin the forward cast just before it straightens. Analyzing the whole cast helps when you're learning, because you can tell when a cast is right, or wrong, simply by watching the loop. A small loop traveling through the air with good speed and power means that your casting stroke is sound and your timing is right. A big, floppy, slow-moving loop tells you that your casting stroke is poor. For safety, keep looking at your backcast even at

Watching the backcast not only helps to improve timing, it prevents serious injury because you will never be hit in the face with the fly.

night. If you always watch the rod tip, your fly or line will never hit you in the face.

The Forward Cast

Timing is critical to making a good fly cast. Beginning the forward cast too soon might snap the fly off the leader; if you begin the cast too late, however, it will fall and hit the ground or water behind you. Waiting too long also causes the cast to lose power. Just before the loop opens, start forcing the rod forward from 1:30 to 10 o'clock. As with the backcast, the tip must travel in a straight line during the forward cast, and the rod must stop cleanly and firmly. Direct the cast slightly upward so the loop opens above the water. Pick a target about 8 to 12 feet above the water's surface and push the cast toward it. Be sure to stop the rod, and don't drop the tip until the line is falling.

If you are right-handed, the rod should stop at about 10 o'clock at the end of the forward cast.

Dropping the rod tip, or forcing the tip down, below 10 o'clock during the forward cast will open the loop and kill your cast. You'll know you're making a good forward cast if the fly line is landing in a straight line in front of you. This is important, particularly in low light, when you want positive line and fly control. If the line lands in a tangled mess and a fish takes the fly, you won't feel the strike because there's too much slack in the line.

FALSE CASTS—ONLY A FEW

Make only several false casts before making your final cast. False casting too many times is tiring and counterproductive, because your fly isn't in the water. One or two false casts should be enough to make a good cast. Once you learn the basic cast, begin feeding out line on your back- or forward cast, and then make your final cast when the rod is loaded with enough line. This is called shooting line. Feed out line by holding it in your noncasting hand, and let it slip out just after making the casting stroke. You'll feel the line pulling in your noncasting hand when the cast has enough power to feed out line.

FIGHTING THE WIND

Don't let the wind be your foe. Use it, don't fight it. Wind blowing into the casting side of your body is the worst, because it drives the line and fly right into you. To counter this, use your backcast to present the fly. It's easy. Simply stand with your back to the water, and use your backcast to present the fly, your forward cast as the backcast. You're just switching the two casts so they're reversed. This technique keeps the fly and line downwind from your body, out of harm's way.

When you're casting into the wind, keep your forward cast low, driving it down into the water. Pick a spot on the water and—trying to keep a tight loop— shoot the line to that spot. Cut back on your casting distance, shorten the leader, and use a smaller fly. Keep your casting stroke the same, but change your casting plane so the backcast is high and the forward cast is low. Do the opposite when you're casting with a wind from your back. Although many anglers feel that a tailwind should be easier to cast with, it's not; in fact, for most anglers it's more difficult, because they don't have a strong backcast. If you're struggling with a stiff tailwind, try using a high roll cast.

THE ROLL CAST

One advantage of the roll cast is that you don't need a backcast. It works well in crowded locations, in confined areas with no backcasting room, and for lifting up sinking line or big flies. And, as mentioned, a roll cast is effective when the wind is from your back.

A roll cast is really a forward cast, but the line is on, or in, the water, and you're using the water's resistance to make the cast. To practice roll casting, you must have water to create resistance. With a floating line, leave about 25 feet of fly line outside the tip. Raise your casting arm just above and behind your head with the rod in the 1 o'clock position. The line must stop moving. Then drive a forward cast using the

This is the proper arm and rod position prior to making a roll cast.

same casting stroke, with the rod tip traveling in a straight line. Pick a spot just above the water and drive the cast toward it.

If you're using a fast-sinking line, you might need several casting strokes, in quick succession to lift the line. With big, heavy flies or poppers, direct the cast higher above the surface to help lift the fly out of the water. Remember, use a normal forward-casting stroke, and stop the rod cleanly.

You can also make your fishing easier by using a roll cast before presenting the fly. Instead of retrieving until the fly line reaches your rod tip, make a roll cast while there's still 15 to 20 feet of fly line outside the tip. Raise your rod slowly and keep working the fly with it until your hand and arm are back in the 1 o'clock position and the fly is near your feet. Make a roll cast, feed out some line while false casting, then make another cast. Using a roll cast helps eliminate excessive false casting. If a fish hits while you're raising the rod, make a hard roll cast; you'll hook most of the fish that strike at this awkward time.

3

HANDLING THE LINE, WORKING THE FLY

Learning to manipulate the fly line efficiently is important. From casting to retrieving to clearing the line when a fish runs, you're controlling the fly line with your hands. Fly lines have different feels, depending on their type. Floating lines are the coarsest, while sinking and clear lines are much smoother. For hooking fish, floating lines are easier to grip. Some lines get sticky in hot weather, while in cold weather other lines remain in tight coils and are difficult to handle. When purchasing a fly line, be sure to choose one that fits your climate and the varying temperatures of the different fishing seasons. The new Wonderlines work better in a variety of environments.

Keep fly lines clean and stretch them before each use. A dirty line will tangle more often and will stick to your fingers when you're retrieving, causing it to ball up. Mild soap and water will clean off some of the dirt, but a good line cleaner works better. Armor All, the auto tire cleaner, is also a good line cleaner and adds a slick finish, but constant usage will shorten the line's life. Be aware that the coating on the new fly lines should not be treated with certain cleaners; consult the manufacturer's directions before using anything other than mild soap.

Stretching a fly line removes the coils that form when it sits on the reel—and a coiled line can be very

Stretch the line by hooking the loop at the end of the fly line to a fixed object, then pulling the line tight.

difficult to cast. Stretching the line before each use is a good practice. Begin by hooking the loop at the fly line's end to a fixed object, pull off the amount you plan to fish, and pull the line tight. You can leave the leader and fly attached to the fly line. In a boat, you can stretch sections of fly line by grabbing the line with your hands, and pulling apart with your arms.

LINE TWISTS

A twisted fly line is difficult to use. Twisting is caused either by using a fly that spins during the cast or as it moves through the water, or by roll casting repeatedly from one side. Each roll cast puts a half twist in the line. When you're continually using the roll cast, try to alternate by using an off-shoulder roll cast every other time. On some casts, extend the casting arm to your opposite side and roll cast from the opposite shoulder. This will offset the line twist. To remove twists in the line, let it hold in a current or trail behind a moving boat. Be sure to remove the fly before doing this. Casting and retrieving in the water, without a fly, will remove twists, but it takes longer.

TYPES OF RETRIEVES

Anglers employ two types of retrieves when fishing for bass and blues. Both work, so choose the one that feels right for you. The first retrieve involves holding the rod with your casting hand, pinching the line to the handle with your first finger, and pulling sections of

This angler is using a single-handed retrieve.

HANDLING THE LINE, WORKING THE FLY   **31**

line using your noncasting hand. This is the primary retrieve used in fresh water. It lets you make longer pulls, use the rod to add action to the fly, and keep the rod in your casting hand so you can present the fly quickly if you suddenly see a fish you want to cast to. Some anglers also like to use the rod to hook fish.

I retrieve with two hands, tucking the rod under my casting arm and taking in line with a hand-over-hand motion. This method allows a faster retrieve as well as a greater variety of retrieves; it lets my casting hand rest; plus it does not cut grooves into my first fingers with the fly line. It also gives me two hands to clear the line once a fish is hooked and, I feel, gives a more positive hook-set. Hooking a fish with just your hands

This angler has the rod tucked under her arm and is using a two-handed retrieve. This method allows for a faster retrieve.

allows you to pull the hook directly, and it won't take the fly out of the strike zone if the fish misses the fly.

How to Work the Fly

Develop a variety of retrieves to make the fly move at different paces. One retrieve that works well is moving the fly at a steady speed. Keep the fly flowing through the water without a pause. The speed can vary from slow to fast, but maintain that speed once you start retrieving the fly. I find that a two-handed retrieve works well for keeping the fly moving at a steady pace.

A pulsating retrieve is very popular, particularly when fishing weighted flies or using sinking lines. You want to make the fly hop, bounce, and dance by using crisp, sharp pulls. There are many variations on this technique. Use different pull lengths, use different speeds, and vary the pauses between the pulls to develop a repertory of retrieves. Examples of different ways to pulsate a fly include a short, quick pull at a steady speed; a medium-length pull with a long pause; and a long, hard pull with a fast retrieve. The variations are endless. Develop and practice several that you can do so well that you don't have to think about them. For night fishing develop a slow retrieve that

At times, a steady, flowing fly is just what the fish are looking for.

you can do even when you're half asleep. In following chapters, I'll suggest the best retrieves to use in different conditions.

After you've learned several steady retrieves, try developing one that changes the beat or strip length of the fly with each pull. This will take more practice, but it works well at times when fish are picky. I seldom use a planned pattern with this retrieve. Instead, I try to mix up different pull lengths with various speeds and pause lengths to create a random fly movement.

Most saltwater fly fishing is blind fishing—you're covering water that looks inviting while searching for fish. The key is covering the water. You want to get the fly to flow through the most productive-looking water while making it look enticing to the fish. Making the fly look alive, or making it look like a crippled baitfish, will excite fish. When fish are feeding heavily, they should take the fly fairly aggressively unless the bait school is so thick that your fly becomes lost in the melee. You need to learn when to apply different retrieves in different types of water, and which retrieves are best with different fly and line types. Trial and

Try changing both strip length and length of pause when retrieving, to give the fly a different action.

error is how most anglers learn. Eventually, you'll be able to do this instinctively. A good way to study fly action is to fish in clear water with bright flies. Experiment with different lines and flies to see how they move with different types of retrieves. This will help when you're fishing in low light or discolored water, when there are no visual aids.

4

HOW TO HOOK, FIGHT, AND LAND
STRIPED BASS AND BLUEFISH

Stripers and bluefish live and feed in similar waters. Stripers are more adaptable than bluefish, however, and tolerate conditions that would drive other species away from an area.

The striped bass (*Morone saxatilis*) is a thick-bodied fish with large fins, a big tail, a good-sized head, and large scales. This fish is built to rummage in heavy water around structure. Its dorsal, anal, and pectoral fins have sharp spines, and you should avoid contact

Stripers have heavy scales, solid bodies, and wide tails.

with them. There are seven dark stripes running later-
ally along the body; the color is olive to dark green on
top with a shiny side and white underside. The fish's
back becomes a light olive over light-colored sand bottoms. The striper's mouth has a rough sandpaper finish; you can grab the lower lip when landing one.

The bluefish (*Pomatomus saltatrix*) is built a little
slimmer than the striper, with a forked tail and a set of
teeth that can sever a finger. Bluefish have a mean
look, and will actually try to bite your fingers when

Bluefish have sleeker bodies than stripers, and forked tails.

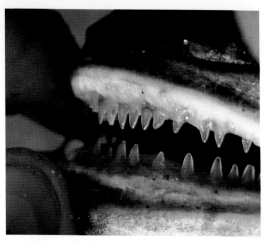
Bluefish have extremely sharp teeth, and powerful jaws.

you're handling them. Hook removal should always be done with pliers. The color is blue-green on the back with a silvery white underside. They have smaller fins than stripers, and while the dorsal fin has spines, it's not nearly as fierce as a striper's. Bluefish won't tolerate as much suspended sand in the water, or as much fresh water, as stripers do. Blues do venture into shallow water, but not with the frequency of stripers. However, they do take a fly more aggressively in skinny water.

The two fish feed on the same foods, the only exception being that stripers will feed more often on

Bluefish are extremely aggressive feeders. This fish, though totally stuffed with baitfish, took a fly anyway.

smaller baitfish and foods such as shrimp and crabs. Stripers make longer runs and are warier than bluefish. Blues, on the other hand, are stronger—fighting like bulldogs when they turn sideways in a rip—and are great jumpers in shallow water. They're also much more aggressive feeders than stripers; they're perhaps the fiercest-feeding fish you'll ever encounter.

The ideal water temperature for fishing both species is the mid-50s to high 60s. Stripers will tolerate colder water, feeding in temperatures down to the mid-40s, but they're slow moving then, feeding near the bottom. Bluefish will feed actively during the day in higher water temperatures. Once the water reaches the mid-70s, stripers feed mostly at night.

The First Strike

Because these two species are similar, the process of hooking, fighting, and landing them is the same. The only major difference is the cutting power of the bluefish's mouth and teeth. Use a bite guard in front of the fly to protect the leader from their teeth. And, as mentioned before, handle blues with great care when removing the hook; it's not just the sharp teeth you have to respect, as their jaws are extremely powerful too.

There are two ways to set the hook when a fish takes the fly. Some anglers like to use the rod itself, lifting or pulling upward with it to drive home the hook. The problem with this is that most rods have too much bend for good hook-sets; they might break if the set is too hard, or if they're lifted too high in the air. When hooking with the rod, you'll also pull the fly away from the fish if it misses its strike. If you want to use the rod for the hook-set, pull it straight back, not upward, while simultaneously pulling the line with your noncasting hand. This creates a straight pull between you and the fish, and won't take the fly out of the fish's feeding range if it misses.

I retrieve with two hands. The rod is under my arm and is never part of the hooking process. When a fish takes the fly, I just keep taking in line, hand over hand, until the line tightens. Then I set the hook with one good pull. Using two hands and a continuous retrieve, I can adjust to any situation for positive hook-setting. Even if I have a large bow in the line, I can easily take in 10 to 15 feet of loose line to set the hook. Doing this while holding the rod with the hand is actually more difficult. When a fish takes with a short, tight line, I can immediately feel the resistance with two hands and soften the pull. When holding the rod with your hand, you must commit to a hard pull at the first sign of a fish.

A sound habit to form is to always follow the line with the rod tip. The rod and fly line should be in one straight line. If the fly line and rod are straight, there is less slack, and you'll have a more positive hook-set. When fishing from a boat, keep the rod down in the water if possible, to eliminate most of the slack.

CLEARING THE LINE

After hooking a fish, you need to clear the loose line that's either in your stripping basket or on the boat

When a fish strikes and runs, grip the line softly to control the flow until the line is running off the reel.

deck. This is a critical time in the fight, so be careful. If the fish runs, hold the line softly and let it slide through your fingers so it doesn't fly about. Never hold the line tightly. Here again, the two-handed retrieve has the advantage, because you have two hands to control the line.

After clearing the line, raise the rod to about a 45-degree angle so there's good bend in it and let the fish run. If the tip half of the rod is straight as the fish runs, the rod is at the proper fighting angle. Try palming the reel's spool to slow the run. Do this carefully at first until you learn how much pressure to apply. Remember, reach for the spinning spool with an open hand, palm first. Keep your knuckles away from the spinning handle if you're using a direct-drive reel.

As the fish runs, hold the rod low, at about a 45-degree angle, and keep it angled to the side, not straight up and down.

Cup the spinning spool to apply more drag. Note that the hand is open and the palm is used to reach for the reel handle.

PUMPING THE FISH

Once a fish stops running, begin pumping it back in. You pump a fish by raising the rod, moving the fish toward you, then lowering the rod and reeling in the loose line. You must keep raising and lowering the rod, and keep reeling to pump in the fish. A large-arbor reel makes this much easier.

If you're fishing from the shore, back up and slide the fish onto the beach once it's close. If you're wading out from the shoreline, raise the rod, bring the fish near you, then grab the leader. With a striper, reach in, grab the fish's lower lip, and hold it firmly. Once you grab the lower lip, the fish will usually freeze. With a bluefish, grab the fish's tail and turn the fish over. This

Bring in the fish by pumping, raising and then lowering the rod while reeling in the line that you gained.

should calm the blue and make handling easier. Use the same technique from a boat.

BARBLESS HOOKS

It's wise to use barbless hooks. They're easier to remove from a fish or from yourself, plus they penetrate much better: With the barb flattened, there's less hook surface to drive into the fish's jaw.

LANDING AND RELEASING THE FISH

When you're landing a small fish, raise the rod, pinch the line to the rod handle with your first finger and pull in the fish using your noncasting hand to take in line. This is the same way freshwater anglers land small trout.

Fish are easier to release if they're landed aggressively. Stripers are hardy, and will come back to life even when exhausted if you take the time to revive them properly. Hold a striper by the tail and keep pushing it back and forth in the water. Use the same technique with a bluefish, but be more aggressive. Bluefish are not as durable as stripers, and you must get them back swimming quickly. Be sure that the fish swims from your hand before letting it go. You'll feel it starting to kick, and it will usually bolt from your grip. The key to releasing fish is landing them quickly and getting them back into the water promptly.

5

FISHING DIFFERENT TYPES OF FLIES

Stripers and bluefish feed on many foods, with active baitfish such as sand eels, silversides, anchovies, and big-sided baits like herring and menhaden making up a good portion of the menu. I'll cover specific patterns and baits later, but this is a good place to discuss basic fly types.

Although some flies copy certain baits, many are attractor flies that look like several food sources rather than one type of bait. Many attractor patterns simulate baitfish, but might also look like a worm or an eel to the fish. Most attractors have flowing materials; this gives them movement even when they drift motionless in the water. I like flies with active materials because they look alive, and they have great movement when a pulsating retrieve is employed.

ACTIVE MATERIALS

Flies made with active materials such as saddle hackle, marabou, and ostrich herl work with many different retrieves. In calm water, a fly with a spun deer hair head and active materials in the wing works well, particularly in low light. Fished with a clear-tipped line and long pulls, the fly leaves a wake, dips down, then bobs back to the surface like a crippled baitfish.

Several flies with active materials.

This fly can also be effective at night when fished with a slow, crawling retrieve.

Flies with spun deer hair heads are also effective when used with a fast-sinking line, because they keep nosing up toward the surface. This up-and-down motion again makes the fly resemble a crippled baitfish. Make medium to long pulls, with a long pause between each, to let the fly wiggle, nose up, toward the surface. Work bigger flies that suggest herring or menhaden in the same manner. Most of the time I fish bigger flies on a sinking line, working them fast with long, hard pulls to make them bolt.

Letting flies with active materials move with the water's flow is another deadly tactic. Try letting the fly swing with the current, adding short pulls without

Fishing with fast sinking line will allow a buoyant fly to rise up toward the surface after each strip.

bringing in any line. In strong currents, a fly that drifts with the flow like this can sometimes bring fish up from the bottom. In some moving water, there are times when letting a fly drift with no retrieve is the only effective way to present it. Dead drifting—getting the fly to swing and turn up current on a tight line—is also very effective.

Another deadly technique is to fish small to mid-sized active flies at different speeds with an intermediate fly line. This also works with small to midsized

Small epoxy flies have little action, but can be extremely effective when they are fished correctly.

epoxy flies. Some small flies have little action; they look very lifelike, but their only movement is what you give to them. Sometimes small, bright flies are effective when fished with a fast, darting action. Epoxy flies look stiff in the water; they're most effective when moving because they look alive. However, they can also produce strikes when drifted below a school of baitfish, because they look like dead bait sinking to the bottom. Big bass often cruise below schools of feeding bluefish, picking up the pieces, so you're just as likely to hook a striper as you are a blue.

POPPERS

Topwater fishing for bluefish is fun and exciting. Getting the popper to generate a lot of noise and commotion is the key. A fast-moving bug is very effective

Several different types of surface poppers.

on blues, particularly in rough or choppy water when a fly might become lost in the surface commotion. Top-water bugs are most effective in calm water, or when a slight wind chop highlights the splash they make. On calm water, in low light, pop a big bug slowly, then let it sit for several seconds before moving it. Smaller bugs can also be effective in calm water when re-trieved with a steady *pop-pop-pop* motion.

WEIGHTED FLIES

The Clouser Minnow is a very popular weighted fly pattern. The lighter ones are especially good flies for beginners, although some have eyes that weigh more than ¼ ounce. These heavy flies are hard to cast, do not suspend in the water column, and can be difficult to use. Heavily weighted flies can also damage fly rods if they strike the rod during casting.

Still, weighted flies are effective because they hop like bucktail jigs. When retrieving a weighted fly, use

A weighted Clouser.

hard, short pulls with a slight pause between each. Try different speeds and pull lengths; the longer the pause, the bigger the hop. Too long a pause will cause missed strikes, because the fish will take the fly on the drop and you won't feel the hit.

BOTTOM FLIES

Two fishing methods work well when you're casting a crab, shrimp, or sand eel fly to a sighted striper in shallow water. One is to allow the fly to sink, then wait for the fish to attack it. After presenting the fly, let it settle; a fish may take it as it drops or settles on the bottom. If a fly moves too much, it can spook a fish. The other method is to let the fly sink, then hop it along the bottom when the fish approaches. At times one hop can be very effective; again, too many moves can scare off fish, particularly bigger stripers.

6

FINDING FISH

How do I find a good place to fish? This is perhaps the most common question I hear at my fly-fishing clinics. The sea is large, intimidating, and confusing for the beginner. The major problem is that most locations will have some fish activity at different times, but determining the better places takes some research. The best time to scout a location is during low tide with an overhead sun. Look for structure, deep holes, cut banks, depressions, and any pockets or deeper sections that might hold gamefish or bait. Try

Look for fish anywhere, even along a harbor channel. Note the boat wake as the angler fights the fish. Several boatloads of anglers passed by, never realizing they were near feeding fish.

to determine how the water flows at different phases of the tide. Look for baitfish and bottom foods such as shrimp and crabs. To learn a place well, visit it at different phases of the tide and different times of year.

Scouting while fishing is another smart way to learn new locations. Watch other anglers, and see what they're doing. I research the outer beaches of Cape Cod by checking the bait anglers. The beaches that have a concentration of anglers fishing the bottom often have good runs of fish. Keep a log of your observations, too. Note the weather conditions, water and air temperatures, sea conditions, type of bait or fish activity in the area, types of flies and line being used, and what success you had (if any). Keeping a good log over the years will help you predict fish activity, and make you a better angler.

Look for Action

First, look for obvious signs such as feeding fish or bird activity. On a calm, early morning, watch for swirls or splashes on the water's surface that could be feeding fish. These signs show up well on smooth surfaces. At night, the sounds of feeding fish will carry a long distance. Take your time; stop, look, listen, and sniff the air for odors of fish or bait. The smell of bait or fish can be strong and has led many anglers to good fishing action.

Watch the birds, as their sharp eyes miss nothing. Small birds like terns will flutter, dive, and swirl over feeding fish. When terns are excited, they're usually

Small terns feeding over fish in fast moving water. The bait is probably sand eels, spearing, or tiny bunker.

over feeding fish; when they're only casually diving, they're picking up baitfish that are on or just below the surface. Small birds are mostly picking small baits. Big birds like gulls cannot catch small baitfish, so if they're actively feeding in the water it usually means

Bigger birds over bigger baits in shallow water.

fish are feeding on bigger baits; they're picking up the pieces. The only time when big gulls can catch small bait is when gamefish drive them onto the shore. Bird activity helps you find fish and can give a hint as to which fly size and type to use. Watch closely to see the size and type of bait that the birds are picking up, then match it with a fly.

LOOK FOR BAIT

Good fishing locations have food. If you find concentrations of bait in a location that has moving water, keep returning there. Sand eels burrow into the sand at night and pop up at first light. Walk into the water along a beach or on a flat and stamp your feet. If little thin fish jump into the air, there are sand eels holding in the sand. Come back to this spot at first light, as a

Spearing are important baits for the fly rodder.

feeding frenzy may occur when the baitfish leave their hiding spots.

Look for silversides along a shoreline, or along the grass banks of a marsh. In spring, these small baitfish spawn up inside estuaries. Many marsh systems have good schools of silversides that attract feeding fish. Look for fish—mostly stripers—to drive these baits against the grass banks to feed.

Bigger baits such as herring and alewives also move into some estuaries, to spawn up inside the tributaries. Stripers will be waiting when these big baits leave the spawning areas. Watch the marshes in May to early June for hot fishing activity when the gamefish will trap big baits along marsh banks. This is a good opportunity for catching big stripers on a fly.

THE WORM HATCH

Estuaries also have swarms of both small shrimp and worms that attract stripers. One exciting event is the "worm hatch," which occurs in spring to early summer. Small red to orange to brown *Nereis* worms typically appear around the new or full moon when big tides occur. Flat, hot, calm weather is the best time for good hatches. The surface will be covered with 2- to 4-inch-long worms that swim around in circles. Many locations have swarms at night, but some places have afternoon or morning activity; it depends on the area. These hatches are not always predictable, and you must do some searching to find good fishing.

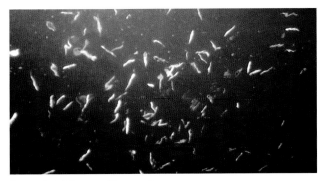

A worm hatch is an exciting event.

The 2- to 4-inch worms begin to change color from bright red to brown/tan at the end of the hatch.

LOOK FOR SLICKS

A telltale sign of fish or bait activity is a slick—a shiny, oily section of water that shows up as a calm spot on a wind-chopped surface. Herring, alewives, and menhaden are oily baitfish and usually leave a good, heavy slick if they're in an area. Small slicks that well up in spots might be feeding fish. Feeding bluefish cut baitfish to pieces and create slicks that form quickly, starting as a tub-sized oil spot that keeps growing as the wind spreads the slick. Slicks along a beach or next to a jetty might mean there's a good supply of bait, but not necessarily feeding fish. All species of baitfish will create some type of slick.

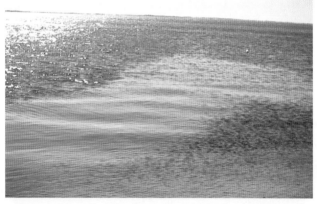

A slick, or calm, oily spot on the surface, might suggest both the presence of baitfish and feeding gamefish.

SOME GOOD PLACES TO FISH

Estuaries

Estuary mouths are perhaps your best bet if you're fishing a location for the first time. Smaller ones are easier to fish and require less research. Outgoing tides force the bait from sheltered areas, out to waiting game-fish. These outflows on a falling tide, at first light, can produce excellent fishing, as can the areas near them. Lobsterville Beach on Martha's Vineyard in Massachusetts is one example of a big bowl with a good-sized estuary flowing into one end. The area encompasses several miles of easy-to-walk shoreline, along with a large backwater. It's probably the most popular fly-fishing beach in the world, producing excellent results for many anglers. It gets heavy pressure, but anglers keep coming back because the fishing is so good.

Lobsterville Beach on Martha's Vineyard, Massachusetts, offers excellent wading; obviously, the fishing is very good.

Beaches with deep water near shore are ideal gamefish hangouts, and offer easy fishing for the beginner.

Beaches

Beaches with deep reachable water near shore often hold fish. Look for a good slope that drops off into 6 to 10 feet of water depth, 50 feet from shore. If a shoreline like this holds bait, it will produce fish on the incoming tide, and during the first several hours of falling tide. Beaches like this, with gravelly bottoms comprised of small, pebble-to-fist-sized stones, frequently have good supplies of baitfish like silversides and sand eels.

Shorelines

Shorelines with good structure and current flow provide holding areas for both stripers and bluefish. The structure also holds baitfish and crabs. When there's flowing water, gamefish sit behind the structure and

Smooth, sandy beaches are easy to walk and wade; they are ideal for night and low-light fishing.

ambush the baitfish as they swim by. If the area is deep enough to provide holding water with breaking surf, there can be excellent fishing around the edges of the white water. Usually a depth of 10 feet or more near the shore is necessary to give shelter to feeding fish in rolling surf. Some locations with rocky structure that you can stand on have water depths of 20 feet or more right at your rod tip.

Clear Water

In clear-water locations, flats at the edges of drop-offs are good places to look for fish activity. On incoming tides, fish will move from the deeper water into the shallows looking for food. These places are good for sight fishing. Look for fish to frequent these areas in spring and early summer in particular. If you hit the fish—especially stripers—when they first move in after migrating, the action can be hot. Once the fish see too many flies, though, they get picky.

Surf

Open ocean beaches with surf have good runs of fish in both spring and fall. Avoid beaches with surf that's more than 4 feet high; bigger surf is tough to handle, especially for the beginner. Look for a sand- or gravel bar angling out from the beach, or a bar running parallel to the beach that's within casting range of shore. Watch the white water as it breaks over the bar. If this white water rolls over the bar and disappears quickly, there's a hole just behind the bar. Such holes behind bars are excellent feeding locations, and the fish usually feed aggressively there. Even the shore-line of a beach can have good fish activity if the slope is steep. The last two hours of the incoming tide through the first two hours of the outgoing is the most productive time.

Points

If the wave action is light, shallow points along a beach are excellent feeding areas. Stripers will feed right in the white water or along the edges in shallow water. Bluefish usually don't get right into the wash, but they'll feed along the outer edges of the white wa-ter. The white water along a beach confuses the bait and makes feeding easy for gamefish, thus providing easy fishing for the angler. The fish need to strike quickly at any movement, and seldom have the time to look carefully at a fly.

Jetties

Jetties are great places to fish because they allow the fly rodder access to deep water with a short cast. There are many jetties at the mouths of estuaries where fish will feed, literally, against the rocks, right at your feet. Bigger jetties along open beaches can hold big fish when the weather gets nasty. The rock structure provides shelter for baitfish on the lee side, and gives you a place to hide in bad weather.

7

FISHING SLOW WATER

Your first attempts to fly fish for blues and stripers should occur in ideal conditions. Wadable beaches and estuary river systems usually offer such conditions. Choose water that's calm and slow moving; if you're wading, be sure the bottom is flat and smooth. Avoid fishing in strong winds, or in places that require long casts. Use a floating or slow-sinking intermediate fly line that's easy to pick up and cast, and fish with small, easy-to-handle flies. Large, wind-resistant flies and heavily weighted flies are difficult to cast.

Fishing from a boat should be easier, and the techniques are nearly the same. A boat is an advantage because it allows better access to deeper water, plus it has a higher casting platform. Be careful and be quiet; poor boat handling and excessive outboard noise will spook fish in some locations. Anchoring in a flow works better for most novices; the current will help keep the line straight.

CASTING AT DIFFERENT ANGLES TO THE FLOW

Try fishing just after first light along a beach, or anchoring on a deeper flat or along a marsh bank with slow-flowing water; these are ideal settings for your first outing. Begin by stretching the line and putting it into the stripping basket, then wade out carefully (if

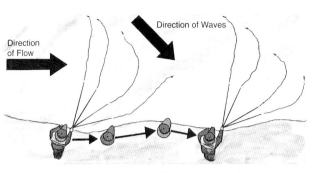

When fishing along a beach, cast at different angles to the flow to cover more water. Work the fly close to the shoreline, particularly at night.

you're fishing from shore) and begin casting. Boat anglers will use the same technique, but the casting direction might be toward shore. As you retrieve, watch the angle of the line to judge the speed of the flowing water. Let's say the flow is from right to left, and that you're making a 50-foot cast straight out, perpendicular to the shoreline. The cast's direction is 12 o'clock. As you begin a slow retrieve the line drifts to the left, and at the end of the retrieve it's at 11 o'clock. To cover this type of water, you need to cast at different angles to the shoreline. In a slow flow the fish are probably moving, but even in slow water the casting angle might be critical. Casting on an angle down the flow keeps the line tight and gives the most positive feel to the fly; this is a better casting angle for most beginners. A cast that angles into the flow will let the fly settle down into the water column, but it also requires more attention, because the line and fly are moving slightly toward you. When casting up into the flow, you need to use a faster retrieve to keep pace with the flow. The novice is wise to begin with a cast that quarters downcurrent.

In a slow flow, try different retrieve speeds to make the fly move at different angles. In slower water, I usually use a faster retrieve unless I want to work the bottom. Even then, I like to fish an intermediate line and let it sink with no movement; once the line and fly have settled, I move the fly quickly along the bottom. If you're fishing a weighted fly with a floating line and want to fish deep, cast upcurrent and let the fly swing well down the flow before retrieving. This will get the fly down for only a short swing before the floating line and current action lift it toward the surface. To reach fish in deeper water, however, a sinking line is clearly the best choice. A floating line, even with a weighted fly, is simply ineffective for reaching fish down deep. Especially in a fast flow, there is no chance to reach the bottom with a floating line unless the fly weighs several ounces.

WHEN TO MOVE, WHEN TO HANG TOUGH

If the flow along the beach runs for several hundred yards, keep casting and moving with the flow. Make several casts, all downcurrent at different angles to the flow, and keep moving down the flow, fishing carefully. Move at a steady pace until you find fish, then fish hard until the action stops. When you're fishing from a boat, keep letting out anchor line or drifting until you find fish. They might be spread out along the shoreline, or they may be holding in pockets. Slow-flowing water usually won't hold fish for very long. Some anglers like to hang in one spot and let the fish find them, but I prefer to keep moving until I find action. Sometimes I'll fish a section of beach, then walk back up and fish it again with a different fly or line.

If there has been recent action along a section of beach, keep fishing it. Last spring, during a school, one student took a good striper because he continued to fish even after the action had stopped. While most of the students and I were gathered around a big summer flounder that another angler had taken, there was a yell from the beach. The angler's partner yelled, "Lou, you'd better get down here quick!" Reaching the two anglers, I saw a bent rod and only backing pointing out to a big dorsal fin and tail on the surface a football field away. The angler played the fish well, but it pulled free just before it was beached. I was standing out from shore, about 5 feet from the fish, when it pulled free. The fish just hung there, not moving, so I knelt down, took it by the nose and tail, and held it for the angler. The fish was tired and froze in my hands. We took some pictures and released the fish. It was only the angler's second striper on a fly, and it weighed perhaps 25 pounds. That's a lifetime striper from shore on fly tackle.

FISHING IN LOW LIGHT

Slow-flowing water is ideal for night fishing. Fish move closer to shore at low light and during darkness. At ease in shallow water during these times, they start feeding more actively. Stripers—even big ones—become different fish at night, and will take flies aggressively. The dark nights around the new moon are my favorite times for fishing, but bright nights can be good and are the best times to learn. Bright nights help most anglers feel at ease. Once your eyes adjust to the low light, you'll be surprised at how much you can see. I've actually been able to spot fish on light-colored, shallow sand flats under a bright full moon.

Begin fishing while there's still ample daylight to be sure that conditions are favorable. The last part of day-

Choose bright nights or places that have a lot of backlighting on your first night-fishing outing.

When planning a night's outing, get to the spot early. The fishing can be hot, and you will become acclimated before it gets dark.

light is a productive fishing time, and you can become familiar with the surroundings and check the water for baitfish.

Use lights sparingly, as they scare fish. But don't sacrifice safety; use a light to find your way rather than risk taking a bad fall. Be careful not to shine a bright light into your eyes, as it might take up to half an hour for them to readjust to the darkness. Serious night anglers use a small dull or red light to change flies. When I change flies, I shine the light into my waders to avoid flashing unwanted light about.

Move slowly, and wade only in locations with smooth bottoms until you're comfortable fishing in darkness. Places with fixed backlighting, such as docks and beaches near roads with streetlights, are good spots for beginners. Stationary lights don't bother fish, and they attract baitfish.

Casting will be tough. Without visual references, you must feel the line in the air to get the proper timing. Some anglers overload the rod by a line size or two so they can feel the rod working with a short cast. There will be nights when a 25- to 30-foot cast is enough to catch fish. Shorten the leader, use a small fly, and watch the backcast to protect your face. Once you learn to feel the line, you'll find that it isn't difficult, and the fish will help because they take flies positively. Never try to fish more line than you can easily cast. The line should slap the rod at the end of most of your casts. This will assure a straight cast and keep clearing the line from the basket. Once you have a

Bluefish also feed voraciously at night; beware when handling fish until you know what species it is.

straight, positive line to the fly, feeling strikes won't be hard. A straight-line cast is essential for night fishing, too. A slow retrieve works best for most night fishing, but I like to mix up the retrieve at times when the fishing is slow. At night, small baits generally swim with a stop-and-go motion, while squid glide and make long pauses. Some baitfish hold and move very little, so a very slow creep can be effective.

At night, treat every fish as a bluefish until you're sure it's a bass. When landing a fish from shore by sliding it onto the beach, walk sideways, not backward.

8

FISHING FAST WATER

Y ou must be flexible in fast-flowing water. Water depth, current speed, wind, how the fish are feeding, and what bait they're feeding on are just some of the factors that might alter fly presentation. Whether you're fishing from a stationary position or in a drifting boat can also affect the way you work the fly. Keep trying different techniques until you find one that works, and remember to apply the same fly action the next time you encounter similar conditions. The secret is to cast at different angles of the current while alternating the speed and length of your strips. Once you build up an arsenal of retrieves, you'll be successful in many different fishing conditions.

MAKING THE FLY SWING

One effective technique is to make the fly swing, turn upcurrent, and rise toward the surface. Use a fast-sinking line, cast quartering downcurrent, then let the fly and line drift and sink before starting your retrieve. Also try casting at various angles to the flow while letting the line sink and drift farther downcurrent. There are some variations on this—different ways to slip or mend the fly line to get the fly deeper and to make it swing more aggressively—but the basic quartering downcurrent cast works as well as any and is easy to learn.

In fast flowing water, both bluefish and striped bass usually feed aggressively. Sometimes they'll take fast moving poppers. Here, the author hangs on as a big striper tries to take line.

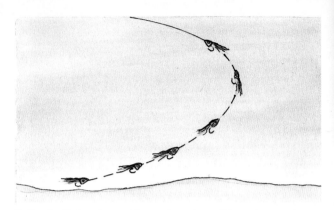

Getting the fly to swing and then swim up toward the surface can be a very effective tactic. Use a fast-sinking line for this.

THE STRAIGHT-DOWNCURRENT APPROACH

If the fish are up in the water column and feeding aggressively, strong current makes fishing easier. In fast-flowing water, fish must strike quickly or they miss a feeding opportunity. The current's speed and the aggressive nature of the fish makes strike detection easier. In some cases you can cast straight down the flow, let the fly make a short swing, hold the line tight, and wait for the take. There are times when just letting the fly sit in the flow produces strikes. With the fly straight downcurrent, the strike is usually hard, with the fish taking the fly positively. Hooking fish should be easy, but don't pull too hard when you feel the take or the line will snap like a rifle shot.

POPPERS IN FAST WATER

When fish are feeding on top, poppers work well and are fun to use. One reason why bluefish are such great gamefish is that they keep charging a popper; sometimes there will be several fish fighting for the same lure. The trick to hooking fish with a popper is to wait until you feel the strike. Attempting to hook fish by watching the splashes won't work, as fish miss poppers frequently. Enjoy the show, but wait for that positive strike before trying to set the hook.

SIPPING FISH

Fish can be tough to hook if they're sipping bait on the surface in flowing water. Try to keep a straight, short, tight line to the fly and feel for every slight touch. Stripers at times will just mouth bait; the take

In slow moving water, fish—particularly stripers—can sip bait in almost a trout-like fashion. The food is usually small and slow-moving when fish are sipping like this.

will be gentle, so you must keep in close contact with the fly. If you have a large bow in the line, be prepared to be frustrated.

GETTING THE FLY DOWN

Fast-sinking lines work well in fast water. In deep locations, use Depth Charge lines to get the fly down to the fish's holding water. If there isn't enough bait to bring fish to the surface, you must get the fly down to the fish. Even when fish are breaking on the surface, fishing deep can be more effective; plus, you have a better chance of taking bigger fish when you fish down deep.

Jetties at the mouths of estuaries, the edges of river-banks up inside the system, and offshore rips can offer similar fishing conditions. The flow can be very strong in such situations, but you still need to get the fly down to catch fish. When you're fishing from a stationary position, with the flow racing by, cast well up-current, then let the fly and line sink and swing well downtide from your position before retrieving. You must give the fly time to get down into the water column. Make the cast upcurrent and wait until the line sinks and swings below your position, then begin retrieving. I generally like a fast retrieve, punctuated with long, sharp pulls. Also try letting the line and fly drift without retrieving; just make long pulls without taking in any line. This lets the fly get deeper and lengthens the swing.

WORKING THE EDGES

Wading can be effective when you're fishing shallow, fast-moving water in low light. In locations with big tides, the edges of flats will flow hard as the dropping water level empties the shallows. The edges of

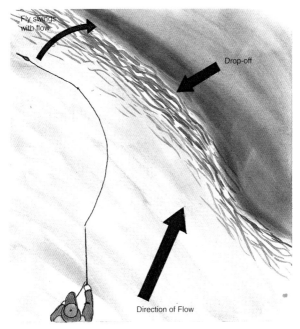

Cast above the drop-off, and get the fly to swing naturally with the flow into the deeper water.

the flats will collect bait and concentrate fish during the last part of the tide.

Stand about 30 feet from the edge, casting so your line and fly swing from the shallow water to the drop-off. Try different swings so the fly flows into the deeper water at different angles. A fast-sinking line is

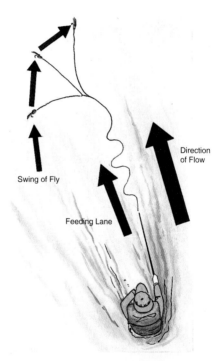

Feeding loose line straight downcurrent can be a deadly technique. This is very effective when you're fishing the edge of a drop-off.

more effective if the flow is hard and the fish are holding deep. An intermediate works well in a moderate flow. When the fish are actively feeding, they will come up, sometimes to the surface, to take a fly.

Try casting almost straight downcurrent as well; after the fly lands, feed out several feet of loose line. Point the rod at the fly and let the fly drift back, make a small swing, and hold in the current for several seconds before you begin a slow retrieve. Do this at different locations in the current, feeding different amounts of loose fly line from 2 to about 8 feet so that it drifts back into the drop-off. The fly will flutter back like a crippled baitfish and come to life as it hits the deeper water. Most of the time you'll have a straight line to the fly, so strike gently.

Use these techniques for fishing shallow reefs or bars, and anywhere that a fast current flows into a drop-off.

9

SPECIAL TYPES OF WATER AND
HOW TO FISH THEM

There are a variety of different water types to fish.
Following are some of the most productive and
most common. Throughout this book I mention certain
fishing conditions and different water types; here I
give you more detail and more precise fishing techniques for some of my favorite fishing waters.

FISHING SHALLOW FLOWING WATER
FROM A BOAT

Drifting in a boat is an effective way to fish 3 to 10
feet of fast-moving water. Big flats hold large numbers
of fish that feed as the falling tide moves baitfish from
their protected holding areas. As the water level drops,
gamefish move slowly downcurrent with the tide,
feeding as they move off the flat into deeper holding
areas. Run the boat away from the location you plan to
fish, ease up into the shallow area, and begin drifting
and casting. Pick spots with a good current, and cast at
different angles to the flow. I usually use a fast-sinking
line, but an intermediate will also work. Move the fly
quickly, with long, quick pulls. My favorite patterns
are a chunky white Deceiver and a heavily dressed
olive Snake Fly. If the shallows are large, you must
first find the fish, then keep drifting the same location

until the fish move off with the tide. Look for the subtle rip lines that indicate a slight drop-off. Fish will hold behind the bars in the depressions, waiting for food to move off the flat. Cast above the rip lines, let the line settle, and begin retrieving so the fly flows over the bar, swimming through the hole at an angle. Cover as much water as possible, because the fish might be moving quickly. They might hold for a short time, but they're usually on the move, hitting the baitfish quickly as the water level drops. Fish will quicken their pace near the end of the tide, as they don't want to be trapped in the shallows. You should also watch the end of the tide, particularly in big-tide areas, to avoid being trapped yourself. Some places in big-tide areas will drain out quickly, leaving you high and dry.

WADING THE EDGES

If you have a shallow-draft boat, carry waders and fish along the edges of flats at the bottom of the tide, or walk out to the edges from shore. These areas hold fish in low light, although they're also good locations for sighting fish when the sun is overhead. There might be hot sight fishing in places where the flats are exposed at low tide and along the edges when they begin to dry up. Walk along the flat, staying an easy cast from the edge. Look for fish feeding up on the flat while schools of sand eels are trying to vacate the shallows. I've seen large schools of small stripers feeding like trout as they sipped sand eels trapped on a flat. Stripers will also hold along the edges and pick up

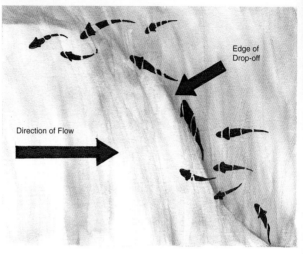

Edge of
Drop-off

Direction of Flow

The edges of flats are good places to find feeding fish, especially
on the last part of outgoing tide.

small baitfish as they spill into the deeper water over
the edge.

FISHING ROCKY CLIFFS

Wave action around structure creates ideal feeding
conditions, particularly for stripers. Bluefish will venture along some cliff sections, usually in deep-water
areas if there isn't too much white water. What makes
fishing along cliffs unique is the way the fish feed in a
location that seems uninhabitable. Coastal sections of
Rhode Island, Massachusetts, and much of Maine have

High rocky cliffs like these often hold fish, particularly when there is white water rolling up against them.

rocky shorelines that hold feeding fish right at your feet.

Some words of caution are necessary before you venture out on rocky cliffs. Never climb down if you'll need to climb back up to avoid breaking waves. Keep away from slippery rocks that angle into the water. Always watch the sea for rogue waves, and move well back from the edge whenever you're changing flies. Watch the spot you plan to fish from for at least five minutes before venturing out. Dangerous times are during big seas and at night. My advice is to fish cliffs only in daylight. Common sense will keep you from getting into trouble. If you don't take chances, cliff fishing is safer than getting in a bathtub.

The best time to learn cliff fishing is in good light, at high tide, with light, 2- to 3-foot seas. Select a section of cliffs that has good footing, with places to land

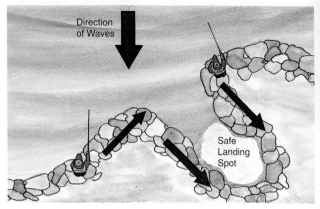

When the surf is large, look for safe places to land played-out fish. A channel, or large crack in the rocks, is an ideal spot.

fish. Look for long cracks in the rocks that extend well back from the heavy surf; these alleys are ideal places for landing fish. The lee sides of points are also safe landing locations. When the waves are big, choose only the fishing locations with good, safe landing spots that you can lead fish into and land them safely.

Most cliffs have deep water right next to the rocks. You can expect to find fish in all the deep pockets, but the best locations are those where billows of white water flow off the rocks into darker pockets of deeper water. These won't look very significant in small surf; in big seas of 5 to 8 feet, though, you might not be able to fish them unless there's a high safe perch close by.

Look for places with cracks and cuts for landing fish.

Working the Flow

Cast as the white water flows back into the sea, letting the flow sweep your line and fly into the deeper water. Keep casting, letting the white water carry the fly to the outer edges of the white water. You must keep working the water so the fly flows out and holds

When fishing along rocky cliffs, look for places where the waves form billows of white water that flow into deeper water.

This is a typical size striper from the cliffs.

at the end of the flow. The white water will dissipate at the flow's end: This is the section of water to keep fishing.

If the waves are small, you can walk along and fish each little pocket, working the wave action around the structure. For smaller surf, an intermediate line is ideal when the fish are up in the water column feeding along the edges of the rocks. In big surf, a fast-sinking line will help get the fly down and will track better in the heavy flow. You can also use a fast-sinking line in small surf to work the deeper holes when the fish aren't feeding up in the water column.

Landing Fish

Landing fish along cliffs is challenging. You must be patient and try to finesse the fish, not outmuscle them. Usually fish don't run; instead, they sound, using structure to hide. If a fish gets around structure, raise your rod up high, putting a full bend in it. Such a full bend puts only slight pressure on the tippet. If the tippet touches the sharp structure with only light pressure, there is less chance of breaking off the fish.

Keep slight pressure on the fish and let the wave action work it away from the structure. Wait the fish out. Many times the fish will swim free after several minutes. With a big fish, you must hope that it swims into open water when it emerges from the structure. To improve your chances of landing fish, use bigger tackle—10-weights, 20-pound tippets—but expect to lose most of the bigger fish anyway. When releasing

Fighting and landing fish from cliffs can be challenging.

Keep the rod high, and with a full bend, if a fish gets behind structure.

fish, walk to a safe spot and slip them into a calm section of water. Because of the wave action, water along cliffs is rich with oxygen and fish generally revive quickly.

OPEN OCEAN BEACHES

Fishing rolling surf is not for the beginner unless the sea is small. The best time to learn how to fish a steep beach is when waves are smaller than two feet. The waves won't have knockdown power, and all the water is fishable. In light surf an intermediate fly line is better for the beginner, and it's the ideal line for fishing in low light or at night. I prefer a fast-sinking line, a 250- to 300-grain Depth Charge when fishing in the daytime. This line is effective when you need to get below

Mixed stripers and blues, feeding just outside the wash.

If you are casting into breaking fish with no success, try working the fly under the thick school of bait.

thick schools of baitfish. In the fall, bass and blues will frequently drive large schools of juvenile herring and menhaden onto the beach. At times you must fish the fly below these schools of bait to have success. If you encounter thick bait when using an intermediate line, be sure to let the line sink for at least a 10-count to get the fly down.

How to Read a Beach

Deeper sections along a beach will have steep slopes right at the shoreline. Look for walls of sand, some 4 to 5 feet high, on the dry section of the beach. These walls mark the deeper holes and holding water near the shore. Many times the walls will be near a

Finding bait such as this along a beach means there is a good supply of food. The fishing should be hot.

point, or a bar that runs at an angle from the shoreline projecting into the sea. Fish and bait collect along these areas, holding in the deeper sections. Two hours on either side of high water is the most productive time to fish most ocean beaches. If you're fishing the bigger, deeper holes—some the size of many football

Author displays a big bluefish that was blitzing the beach along the southern coast of Maine.

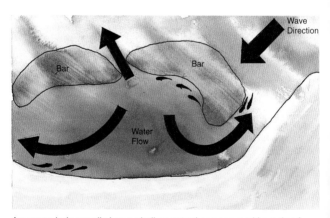

An ocean hole usually has a shallow outer bar or several bars that form a deep pocket next to the beach. Waves rolling over the bars form flows inside the hole that make feeding easier for the fish.

fields—then all tides can be productive. When the surf is big, fly fishing is easier in the bigger holes during the lower phase of the tide.

Fish Close

When the surf is small, blind cast along the beach to cover as much water as possible. Concentrate on the edge where the waves are rolling along the beach. In small surf, I like to cast quartering along the beach, working the edge of the white water. Fish feed right in, or just outside, the white water. The rolling water confuses the bait, and permits easy feeding for both bass and blues. Even big fish will feed right next to the beach; this is an ideal opportunity to take a good-sized fish on fly tackle with only a short cast.

A fish takes a fly right in the wash. When the surf is small and the fish are close, you'll have greater success with a short line.

SPECIAL TYPES OF WATER AND HOW TO FISH THEM   **93**

The wash flowing down a beach creates a perfect feeding environment for both stripers and bluefish.

Last year I spotted several big fish cruising just outside the wash. I quickly walked down the beach and made a cast. Two fish turned and followed the fly, and one of them took. As the fish ran, my fly line knotted momentarily at the first guide, and the tippet parted with a "crack." It would have been the best surf fish I had taken in several years. Big fish have a knack for escaping by the simplest means.

Along ocean beaches you will, at times, encounter strong flows from wave action. Points, as well as different sections of the hole, will have water that is difficult to fish because the fly line is constantly being pushed away from the good holding water. In some cases the only way to present the fly in the best holding water and maintain a tight line is to move with the flow. Keeping the line perpendicular to the shoreline is the key to fishing the fly in the most productive water.

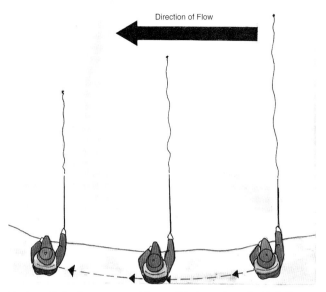

Direction of Flow

Moving with the flow, as you retrieve, will help you keep the fly in the strike zone for a much longer period of time.

After casting, walk at the same speed as the moving water along the beach, retrieving as you walk. This technique will help keep the line and fly from being swept onto the beach by both the flow and the waves.

Keep moving until you find fish. At times there will be concentrations of fish in a few spots along the beach. If you fish only one small section of the beach, you might believe there are no fish there. If the fish are moving, try to keep pace with them as they flow along the shoreline. Watch what other anglers are doing; this will help you determine how the fish are acting. Keep watching the surf line and just beyond.

Fish the Points

Work flowing water around points. The edges on either side of a point are always hot spots. Cast up onto the point and let the fly flow into the deeper water along the edge. At times the shallow water right on the point is good; fish will feed right in the first wave. In

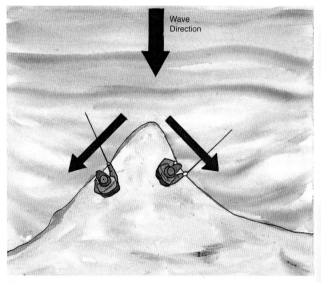

Along ocean beaches, both sides of a point can hold fish unless the waves create too much flow. Let the fly swing with the flow.

Points that protrude at an angle to the beach can be ideal fishing locations. Fish the flowing water along the bar's inside edge.

small surf, keep retrieving if the fly doesn't have enough movement from the flow. If you feel the fly moving at a good pace, wait until it settles into the deeper water before retrieving. This water will be tough to fish if the waves are more than 4 feet high, and impossible in 6- to 8-foot waves.

Any bar that runs from the beach into deeper water might have fish holding, usually along the inside edge. Watch the white water that rolls over the bar. If it spills across the bar and disappears, there's a hole behind the bar. Stand on the bar and cast into the white water, letting the fly flow with the white water so it swings into the hole. Fish should take as the fly flows into the drop-off. Once the fly settles into the hole, retrieve it slowly with short pulls. If that doesn't produce, try

This is the backside of a bar on an ocean beach at low tide. Some bars might have a 5- to 6-foot drop-off behind the bar.

moving the fly quickly. Fish will take the fly aggressively in flowing white water, and are seldom picky about patterns.

Bars that run parallel to the shoreline offer a similar fishing situation. With the bar straight out from shore, cast straight into the white water and bring the fly back toward you. The flow will be moving toward you, making a fast retrieve, at times, necessary to maintain contact with the fly. This can be tricky unless you can retrieve faster than the moving water, and are ready to retrieve as soon as the fly lands.

Use Waves to Land the Fish

Landing a fish of more than 10 pounds in even moderate surf takes some skill. When it's in rolling water

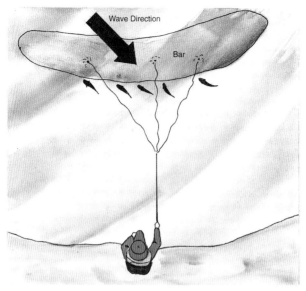

Cast onto the bar and work the fly so it flows with the white water into the pockets on the inside.

that surges up and down the beach, a fish will feel much heavier than it is. Fish use this surging water to their advantage. To land a fish in the wash, you must turn it so its nose is facing the beach. Then punch the fish, nose first, through the wave, and hold the fish from getting back into the wave as it flows down the slope. If the fish remains sideways to the waves, landing is difficult. It might take several tries to accomplish, but be patient and remember that too much pressure will pop the leader. With a big fish, you might

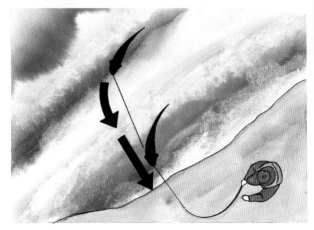

When landing a bluefish or striper on a steep beach, you must turn the fish and punch it headfirst through the inside wave.

walk up and down the slope half a dozen times before you get it inside the first wave. Once the fish is inside that first wave, the next wave should put it high and dry. After hooking a fish, be sure to back up the beach so you're above the rolling waves.

Conditions are ideal for fly fishing when the surf along the steep ocean beaches is less than 3 feet. An increase of 1 foot in wave size increases the fishing difficulty by three times. Beaches with a longer, flatter slope are tough to fish in waves more than 2 feet high, unless you don't mind getting wet and getting knocked around by the surf. When the ocean beaches

Use the wave action along the beach to help land fish.

get big, move to more sheltered water; don't fight tough conditions.

SIGHT FISHING

One of the most difficult yet most exciting types of fly fishing is casting to a sighted fish in shallow water.

Fish like this nice-sized striped bass might be feeding right in the wash, even in broad daylight.

You must spot a fish, calculate its speed and the water's depth and flow, then cast the fly quickly so it settles into the fish's view before the fish sees you.

Being able to spot fish quickly is the first concern. A group of fish usually shows up well over a light bottom, but singles and pairs can be tough unless the water is very shallow. The keys are to look for movement,

Stripers will hold and feed in very shallow, clear water in the daytime.

and to look for the shadow below the fish. Once you learn to see moving shadows, spotting fish becomes easier. Being in a stationary position, either wading or fishing from an anchored boat, will help you see movement. If you're in a drifting boat, you're moving

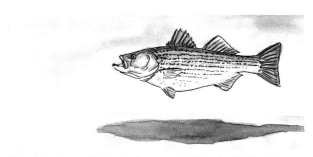

When trying to spot fish in shallow water, look for the fish's shadow; then you'll be able to see the actual fish.

SPECIAL TYPES OF WATER AND HOW TO FISH THEM **103**

too and everything seems to have motion. Unless you're fishing with a guide who can spot fish for you, sight casting from a stationary position makes spotting fish easier.

Casting to the Fish

Wading is also an advantage because you can get closer to the fish. Spotting fish is easier from the height of a boat, but the fish can also see you much better, and the boat makes noise. When you're sight fishing from a boat, you'll often need to make longer casts to avoid spooking the fish. A quiet wader can usually slip to within 25 or 30 feet of a fish.

Most sight casting is done at distances of 30 to 60 feet. The secrets of good sight casting are speed and accuracy. Spotting the fish at a good distance helps, as it gives you time to set up. Most good sight-fishing anglers follow a routine to help the cast and presentation go smoothly: Start with about 10 to 15 feet of fly line outside the rod tip. Hold the fly in your noncasting hand. Now grip the fly line with the first and second fingers of your casting hand, holding it away from the rod. Pinching the fly line to the rod makes it difficult to pick up the line. When you're ready to cast, throw a forward loop, which should pull the fly from your hand. Rather than dropping the fly—it might end up in your leg—let the forward motion of the line take it from your hand. As the fly leaves your noncasting hand, reach over and grab the line between the two fingers of your casting hand and make a backcast. If you

Holding the line between the first two fingers allows you to grab it quickly when you're sight casting.

have enough line speed, shoot some line and decide if you can cast to the fish. Most anglers should make one false cast before casting to the fish. This gives you time to think and helps smooth out the cast. If the fish is more than 40 feet away, you'll probably need the extra false cast.

Never rush the cast. Too many anglers try to hurry and miss opportunities because of it. Go at a comfortable pace and you'll get the fly to enough fish.

Either a floating, clear-tip, or full-clear intermediate fly line will work. Most anglers prefer a floating or clear-tip line because they can judge the distance between the fly and the fish. When you're using a full-length clear line, it's difficult to know how close the fish is to the fly if you lose sight of the fly's position.

My wife, Barb, with a fat striper that took a fly in several feet of water.

Use a 9-foot leader for a floating line and a 3- to 5-foot leader for the clear-tipped or fully clear line.

Don't Move the Fly

After casting to the fish, watch the fly as it settles to the bottom. If the fish is coming to the fly, let your offering keep falling. Stripers will usually hit the fly either as it drops or once it's on the bottom. Adding action to the fly can scare fish, particularly bigger stripers that have seen many flies, so be careful. Bluefish should attack the fly, and will at times take a popper readily.

Keep watching both the fish and the fly to know when to set the hook. Sometimes you'll see the fish grab the fly. The fish's reaction will tell you that it has the fly.

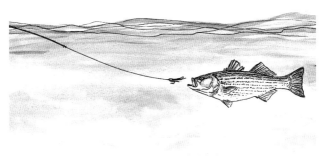

You usually want to present the fly at eye level or below. Stripers seldom look up when they are feeding in shallow water.

Look at the fish's body language to tell if it has taken the fly; the flash of a fish's side is a good indicator.

Stripers take a fly from the bottom by either nosing down or turning on their side. The angler will feel the fly stop abruptly, in either case.

A bluefish takes the fly aggressively; stripers will usually feed cautiously in shallow water in the daytime.

Look for the fish to turn, for a flash of its side, or for it to nose down on the fly. Then hesitate for one second and set the hook by making one long pull, called a strip strike. You can also take in line with a hand-over-hand retrieve if the rod is tucked under your arm.

Bluefish are great sport in shallow water. There are late-summer days in Long Island Sound, at the mouth of the Housatonic River in Connecticut, when the blue fishing is absolutely out of this world. At low incoming tide, the outer bars have pods of fish milling on the sur-

Bluefish are great performers in shallow water. Some fish will put on a real aerial display, and jump five to six times.

face. The water isn't clear but the fish are visible, leaving wakes on the surface. These fish will hit poppers with a vengeance. But they're spooky, and you need to cast well away from them. When a group of fish swims across your path, cast well ahead of their direction of travel so the popper intercepts them. After a fish takes a popper, it either runs and jumps, or just starts jumping. Some fish go airborne half a dozen times. As one angler described it to me, "You could travel many miles and spend big money and not have fishing this good." The only area that might rival the Housatonic is in the Chesapeake Bay, where some good flats in the lower bay offer good sight fishing for bluefish in spring if there isn't too much runoff to discolor the water.

BIG JETTIES, BAD WEATHER

I like fishing jetties when conditions are stormy and fishing is tough in other locations. The jetty must be high enough to offer protection from the wind, rain, and big seas. If the jetty's lee side offers protection from the wind and waves, it's fishable. The only way to check jetties in rough weather is to walk out and see how the water conditions are. From shore it can look worse than it really is. If the water is fairly free of floating weeds and not too riled up, start fishing. Look at the water movement along the jetty. There should be a flow coming from the shore out along the rocky side. Now look for a good safe access spot to fish in that flow.

Pick a place along the rocks and climb down, getting as close to the water as possible while still being safe. Most jetties have small pockets in the rocks that offer protection and a comfortable place to sit or stand. One of the best spots is where the moving water from inside, which flows along the jetty, ends. If there's a good place, begin fishing so you can cover this flow. Even if the wind is strong, all you need is a short roll cast to reach good holding water. The mistake most anglers make is trying to cast too far. Work the water close to the jetty, keeping your casts short to make line control easier. There are times when I'll cast only 25 feet. I've had several big fish take the fly within a few feet of the structure.

Let the fly swing in the flow and come to rest along the edges of the rocks. Allow it to hold in the moving water next to the jetty. The fly will look like a baitfish

Where the jetty meets the beach is an excellent fishing location, particularly at low incoming tide.

trying to hide along the jetty's side. You'll find different types of baitfish, small bottom fish, and even eels hiding inside the structure. Wave action pushes this food out to gamefish that cruise the area, looking for a meal. One of the biggest bluefish I've seen taken from shore—an 18-pounder—took a swimming plug right next to a jetty. The angler thought he had a big striper.

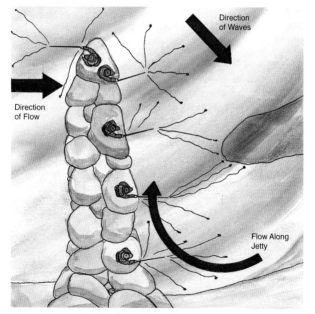

Work all the water around a jetty carefully, casting at different angles to the structure. Let the fly swing in the flow, then come to rest.

The trick to fishing jetties in rough water is to hang tough and keep fishing the same few locations. If the water is working right, fish will keep searching the rocks for food. The best casting angle is often a quartering cast down the flow. Usually a slow retrieve with short pulls works best, although at times I let the line and fly drift with almost no retrieve. The fish will take softly, just a slight tightening of the line. It can be intense fishing, not a time to daydream. Jetties are perhaps the best opportunity for the fly rodder to hook a big fish on a short line.

If you do hook a big fish, the best landing technique is to walk toward shore and fight the fish from the beach. Let the fish run out from the structure while you walk toward shore; then get off the jetty and walk

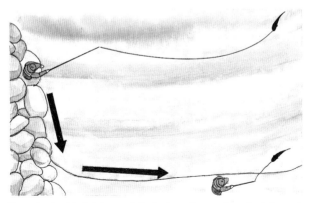

If you hook a big fish from a jetty, try to walk away from the jetty and fight the fish from the beach, where you can land him.

up the beach away from the rocks to land the fish. Trying to land a big fish from rocks is difficult and dangerous, as the only way is to climb down the rocks and try to grab it.

Even in big water, an intermediate line works well and is easy to pick up when making a roll cast. It's the best line to fish in low light. I might try a fast-sinking line in daylight if the water is very heavy, but a slow-sinking intermediate line will make the fly come alive as it holds along the rocks.

BIG OFFSHORE RIPS AND ESTUARY RIVER SYSTEMS

I've already discussed some fishing techniques for deep, fast water, but there are a few other methods that you need to know. You can find excellent fishing on some of the big offshore rips as well as in the rivers and shorelines of big estuaries. Some rips, like the ones around Martha's Vineyard and Nantucket, are all sand, while others, like the Sows and Pigs off Cuttyhunk in Massachusetts, are heavy structure. River systems of estuaries like the Chesapeake Bay, the Hudson River, or the Kennebec River in Maine are mixtures of rock, gravel, sand, and mud. Many of these places are 5 to 40 feet deep with fast-moving water when the tide is at full flow. The heavy ocean rips have stand-up waves, formed because the water depth changes abruptly from several feet to 30 feet or more. The perilous rips are walls that can run almost straight up, pushing the flowing water to a boiling froth. No loca-

Capt. Bob Luce holds a big fish for the camera. The offshore rips can have good numbers of large fish such as this.

tions inside estuaries have dangerous waters like those of an offshore rip, but when they flow into open water, sea conditions can be dangerous.

Leave the really big waters to the professional guides. Some of the heavy offshore rips will swallow a boat unless you're an experienced captain. There are many open rips that you can fish successfully, however. Most of the water inside estuaries doesn't have wave action, but the flows can be strong, particularly around structure.

Use the Motor

On offshore rips, most guides will fish their clients with the motor running, stemming the tide and letting the angler cast to the side or behind the boat. Guides use both stemming the tide and drifting to position an-

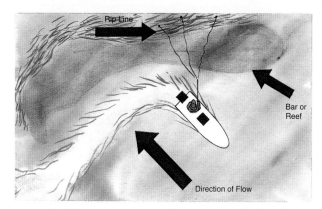

Rip Line

Bar or Reef

Direction of Flow

In tough-to-fish places, use the boat's motor to stem the tide. Then you can work the fish-holding water over a bar or reef.

John Posh, owner of Stratford Bait and Tackle in Stratford, Connecticut, with a bluefish that took a fly just after first light.

glers just above the fish. Putting the boat in and out of gear lets the line and fly settle into the water column and swing to waiting fish. This works well in crowded locations, as it allows many boats to fish one location. Another way to fish a location like this is to shut off the motor above the rip and drift down to the fish. This is a good technique unless the rip has stand-up waves, or if there is structure just below the surface. Some rips are too dangerous to enter when the tide is flowing hard.

Drifting

In locations where drifting with the boat is possible, I like to work the water by flowing downcurrent while continually casting. This is very effective inside river systems, especially when the water is discolored. You can cover more water and go back over the same location several times. Drifting allows you to cover the

If the rip is not too rough, drifting and casting can be productive.

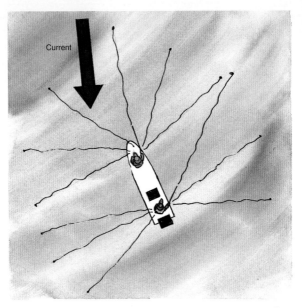

When drifting, try casting at different angles to the current until you find the most productive fishing angle.

water more efficiently, getting the fly deeper and fishing at different angles to the current. When you're drifting in a flow, keep casting at different angles to the current, and try letting the line and fly sink before starting the retrieve. As you retrieve, the line will swing, turning the fly toward the surface as it straightens out.

The boat should drift at the same speed as the current unless the wind is blowing. The fly, in turn, will act like

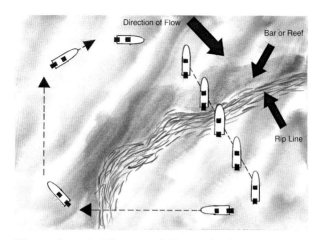

When continuously drifting over a fishing location, be sure to run around the area, not back over it.

a normal baitfish because it's moving with the flow. Use different retrieve speeds and pull lengths, depending on which bait type you're trying to match. If fish are feeding on squid or bigger batifish (4 to 7 inches long), use long, sharp pulls and move the fly quickly. If they're on tiny, juvenile bait, try a slow retrieve with short pulls. If the fish are finning on the surface, use an intermediate line, a small white fly, and a slow retrieve with 3- to 4-inch pulls. If you're fishing a river system, expect to find hatches of small baits like worms, crabs, or shrimp. Match your fly to those baits.

With the boat drifting at the same speed as the flowing water, you can let the line sink and fish the fly deeper. Unless the water is shallow or a specific bait is

Getting the fly down can be critical, especially on bright days.

bringing fish to the surface, getting the fly down will produce more strikes in fast-flowing water. If you're getting the fly down 10 feet in 15 feet of water, the fish might come up this short distance to take the fly. If the fly is on the surface, however, there's less chance of fish rising up that far to take the fly. Besides fish coming up to feed on bait, the only other times you're likely to find fish near the surface are in low light and at times of slack water.

SMALL OPENINGS THAT FLOW INTO OPEN WATER

These are my favorite places to fish. If I could fish only one water type, it would be a creek or small river flowing into deeper water. I like places that you can cast across when the flow spills into 6- to 10-foot drop-offs. Places like this have consistent action, are easy to fish, and usually remain the same for many years.

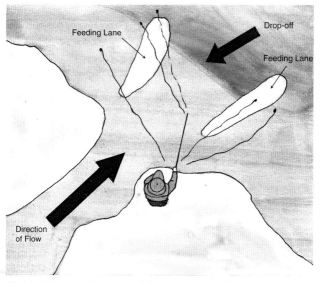

Work both the feeding lanes and the drop-off when fishing outlets.

Openings that run into the sea are great places to fish.

The Best Times to Fish

The first part of the outflowing tide and the first part of the inflowing tide are usually the most productive times to fish estuary mouths. The opening's size and the size of the backwater or estuary will determine how much lag time will occur. The flow won't begin moving out immediately after high water; most openings will have a delay, some up to several hours, before the water begins to run out. The inflow will have the same lag time. Here is where your fishing log becomes invaluable; it can help you predict the most productive fishing periods so you don't waste your time.

Cast to different areas where the flow runs into the drop-off. Fish will often hold along the edges or just behind the drop-off. In a faster flow, the fish will take aggressively when they're feeding on baitfish. Out-flows are grocery stores. As the estuary empties, it dumps food into the open water. The constant flow of food attracts gamefish, because the feeding is easy. A feeding frenzy can occur when there are large numbers of baitfish flowing out; the fish might hit anything that moves. This can be easy fishing. Just cast quartering downstream, then let the line and fly swing while making short pulls with a slow retrieve. Basic attractor flies work well, as do poppers.

When Fish Feed on Small Foods

If the food source is worms, shrimp, or crabs, stripers and blues will mostly be sipping them on or near the surface. You can often determine bait types by watching the feeding styles of the fish. If there are subtle swirls and small rings on the water's surface, the fish are usually feeding on small, immobile baits like spawning worms or shrimp. If the surface activity is loud with large splashes, and fish are crashing on top, they're feeding on fast-swimming baitfish such as herring or spearing.

When the fish are sipping, use small flies and try to cast the shortest line possible without spooking the fish. Cast above the feeding fish and let the fly swing to them on a dead drift. During worm and shrimp hatches, some fish will take up feeding stations like trout in a river, taking food only inside a small window. Even when the bait is thick, you can take fish if you keep putting your fly in that window.

Try to match the fly to the bait type, use a floating or intermediate line, and keep the cast short for better control. Keep in mind that the fish might feed more aggressively if the bait is spread out. Stripers will feed like this more often than bluefish will, but don't be surprised to get cut off by the occasional big chopper bluefish that act like trout.

10

MATCHING FOODS AND FLY TYPES

I like fishing the sea because the flies are usually simple, basic patterns. Some special fly types are necessary for certain fishing conditions, but simple patterns like the Deceiver, the Snake Fly, and the Clouser Minnow will catch fish a good portion of the time. If you have several patterns that are 2 to about 6 inches long, all-black, all-white, and all-chartreuse, you can effectively cover most fishing situations. Blending colors will suggest action and make the fly more lifelike. Plus, it's more fun to tie flies with mixed colors: Solid-colored flies can be boring to work on.

Most of your fly arsenal should consist of attractor patterns tied with materials that move freely in the water. Marabou, saddle hackle, and ostrich herl all impart a breathing action that makes the fly look alive; they keep undulating even when the fly is motionless in the water. Also carry precise patterns in your fly boxes. Epoxy flies, for example, are good for clear, shallow water when fish won't take other offerings. Have a selection of smaller patterns to match sand eels, spearing, and herring-type baits. Add eyes to these flies. In clear water, in particular, a baitfish's eye will stand out prominently and catch gamefish's attention. If you plan to sight fish, have some specific shrimp and crab patterns as well. The active flies should still be your mainstay, however.

WEIGHTED FLIES

Anglers like to fish very heavily weighted flies because they bounce like bucktail jigs when retrieved with sharp pulls. Some fly rodderes just fish with a floating line and heavy lead-eyed flies. They catch fish, but become one-dimensional anglers. I prefer unweighted or lightly weighted flies because they hold in the water column like live baitfish; a fly with too much weight starts sinking as soon as you stop retrieving. Heavily weighted flies have other drawbacks: They are difficult and dangerous to cast, and if they hit the rod during the cast they can fracture the graphite and cause the rod to break. If you're sight casting and want a fly that will settle all the way to the bottom, try using a sparsely tied fly with $\frac{1}{16}$-ounce eyes. Such an offering is heavy enough to settle slowly, but it's not difficult to cast.

There are several important baitfish, or families of baitfish, that you need to know about when fishing for blues and stripers. To keep it simple, there are thin, midbodied, and wide-bodied baitfish. Some of the wide-bodied baitfish are midbodied when they're young, growing into deeper-bodied fish as they mature. Following are the names and importance of the various baitfish, but don't go crazy trying to learn them all. Most beginners need to know only the basics about the foods that gamefish eat. Once you become a better angler, then learning the life cycle and habits of each bait will improve your success rate.

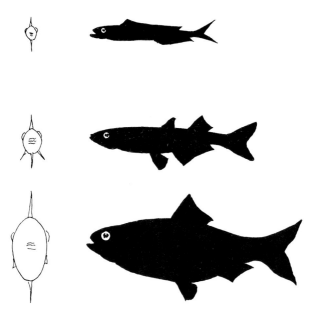

There are three basic categories of baitfish: thin, midbodied, and wide-bodied.

THIN BAITFISH

The most important thin baitfish is the American sand lance, or sand eel (*Ammodytes americanus*). Sand eels grow to 8 inches in length but usually range in size from 2 to 5 inches. Abundant along sandy shores and inside estuaries, sand eels are the only baitfish that burrow into sand to hide or rest, popping out at first light to form big schools. In size and shape they re-

A selection of sand eel flies.

semble a pencil, making them an ideal food to match with a fly. They're a dominant food source from southern Maine to New Jersey. Matching the sand eel is simple: Use thin Deceivers, thin Snake Flies, or sand eel patterns tied with skinny tails and simple, wrapped bodies. The best colors are all-yellow, all-black, or white bottom and purple, blue, or olive backs, tied on No. 4 to 1/0 hooks.

MIDBODIED BAITFISH

The silversides or shiner (*Atherinidae* spp.) and the bay anchovy (*Anchoa mitchilli*) are the major midbodied baitfish. Small herring and mullet are also midbodied until they reach a certain age. Adult shiners spawn in spring and then die; the juveniles grow through the season and are full sized by fall. In spring, look for adult shiners to congregate inside estuaries along the banks and up onto grass-covered shallows, where

The Deceiver is a good pattern for imitating many food types. It works well matching any midbodied baitfish.

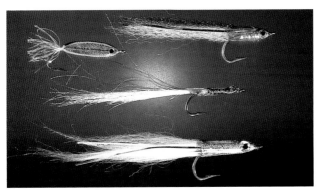

Lifelike epoxy flies are a good match for anchovies, and work well in clear water when fish are picky.

they'll spawn. Shiners have green backs, bright, shiny stripes down their sides, and white undersides. Deceivers, Snake Flies, and Clouser Minnows are all good silversides imitations, tied in all-white, all-chartreuse, or white with green back, 2 to 5 inches long on hook Sizes 2 to 1/0.

Bay anchovies look very similar to silversides, growing to approximately 2½ inches long. The color is similar, but their backs are brilliant green, and might look tan in some waters. Small No. 4 and 2 epoxy flies, 1½ to 2½ inches long, work well when fish are actively feeding on anchovies. I've also had success with small single-winged streamers, tan, mixed with flash and having bright bodies.

BIG, WIDE-BODIED BAITFISH

The big, wide-bodied baitfish all fit in one category. The alewife (*Alosa pseudoharengus*), blueback herring (*A. aestivalis*), Atlantic herring or sea herring (*Clupea harengus*), and Atlantic menhaden, bunker, or pogy (*Brevoortia tyrannus*) are the four important big baits that bass and blues feed on. As adults they range in size from 8 to about 18 inches. Six- to 10-inch-long flies are often needed to entice fish when they're feeding on adult baitfish. Alewives and blueback herring move into estuaries, spawning in freshwater tributaries in spring. The young baitfish form schools, leaving the estuaries in early fall. Big stripers look for the adults early in the season when the baits come back from their spawning activities. The period from May to mid-June is an excellent time to fish big flies in and around estuaries.

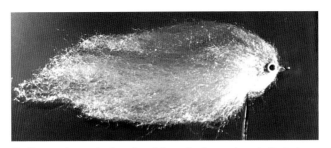

Big flies can be productive when fish are feeding on large baits, but they are hard to cast, especially in even a mild wind.

Menhaden and sea herring spawn in open water, with the larvae moving inshore and developing into 2- to 5-inch-long juvenile baitfish by late summer and early fall. The young of all four of these wide-sided baitfish form into big schools and move south as the water begins to chill. When stripers and bluefish find these aggregations of food, they feed wildly, taking flies very aggressively.

The Deceiver is perhaps the best fly to match these big baits. Make or buy the biggest ones you can cast; 8-inch flies will max out most casters. If you own a 9-weight, try to use flies made with light, water-shedding materials. Tie them sparse, but with wide silhouettes. Only 10- to 12-weight rods will handle the really big patterns if longer casts are necessary.

To match juvenile baitfish, flies in the 2- to 5-inch-long range are most effective. Deceivers and Slab Flies work well, in all-white or white with blue, green, or gray backs with some flash. Use hook Sizes 2/0

Small flat-sided flies are effective in the late summer and into the fall, when the juvenile bunker and herring begin to appear.

to 4/0 for the bigger patterns, 2 to 1/0 for the smaller patterns.

OTHER FOODS

Small bottom baits like worms, shrimp, and crabs are specialty foods. They are important, but these special foods should not consume too much of the beginner's time. All three baits will swarm at certain times, with the "worm hatch" perhaps the best-known event. These swarms attract mostly stripers, but bluefish will at times join in the feeding.

The clam worm (*Nereis* spp.) transforms, swarms, spawns, and dies usually on new and full moons during May through July. The swarms occur mostly at

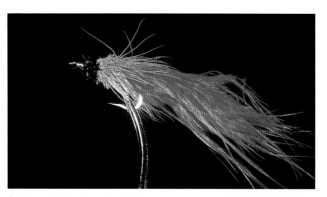

Serious night anglers should also carry some worm-hatch flies in their tackle bag.

night, but in some locations they happen in the morning or afternoon. Calm, warm days or nights without drastic weather changes are the best times to fish. Fish feed heavily in good swarms, but catching them can be difficult. If the bait is too thick, you must get the fly very close to the fish, right on their noses. A fly that leaves a wake is very effective. Snake Flies, all-black (at night) or red, orange, or tan with a dark head, work well. Make flies that are 3 to 4 inches long, on a No. 4 to No. 2 hook. A number of worm patterns, including Dixon's Devil Worm and the Blossom, are also effective.

Crab and shrimp flies work well for stripers in shallow, clear water—especially when the fish are picky feeders. Bonefish and permit flies also work well, on hook sizes from No. 4 to 1/0. Usually they're most

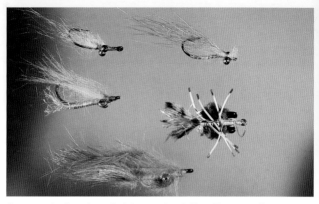

Carry a selection of small shrimp and crab flies. They are effective in estuaries and on the flats for sight casting.

effective when you cast and let them settle to bottom in front of sighted fish.

FISHING TOP WATER

Surface flies and popping bugs are fun to fish, and quite effective, at times bringing fish from great distances. Poppers work well in spring when fish are feeding on silversides along grassy banks. They are also effective for bluefish in shallow water, and will bring stripers up from deep water on calm mornings.

Select a popper you can cast. If you have a 10-weight rod, carry big poppers to make lots of noise and small poppers to use in shallow water. A popper should float well, have a large enough hook, and produce a good splash. I like poppers that I can see, but a dark popper can be effective in low light.

Flies that produce wakes work well on calm nights. Patterns like the Snake Fly, or Muddler-type flies with spun deer hair heads, will push good wakes on the surface. The wings should be made of active materials and tied chunky to float well.

For anglers who want detailed information on the foods that gamefish eat, I can't help but recommend *Lou Tabory's Guide to Saltwater Baits and Their Imitations.*

11

TIDES

The changing of water depth—tide—is a predictable event that occurs each day, with two high tides and two low tides. The tide changes approximately every 6 hours and 12 minutes, with the tide being about one hour later every day. Unlike a river, which needs rain to change its flow, some sections of the sea are constantly moving, either rising or falling. The tide adds movement to the water, making fishing more predictable, giving the angler times when the fish feed more aggressively.

KNOW THE TIDE'S SIZE

Be aware that the tide fluctuates differently in different locations: North of Cape Cod, up into Maine, for instance, the tides are large, changing 9 to 12 feet depending on the moon phase. Yet only 6 to 7 miles away, on the south side of Cape Cod, which includes Nantucket and Martha's Vineyard, tides are less than 5 feet, with some locations having only 2-foot tides. To fish effectively, you must know how much the local tides fluctuate in different areas, because they vary all along the coast.

The current will be stronger in big-tide locations. However, there can be very strong flows even in small-tide places if the water depth changes abruptly.

A location can look different at different tides. Places with big tides will change considerably between high and low tides.

Great Point, Nantucket, has only a 3-foot tide, but the rip that flows over the bar at the point is frightening; the water rises from 50 feet to just a few feet abruptly, and the flow is also blocked by the point, funneling a tremendous amount of water into one small location. Anyplace where the water's flow is constricted—a reef or bar rising sharply from the bottom, a small opening draining a large backwater, or a large point or reef protruding from land—will create strong current.

USE TIDES FOR BETTER FISHING

Tides can help you plan a day's fishing, or the whole year's for that matter. As you begin to learn different locations, you'll discover that certain phases of a tide are more productive and fishing conditions are easier in certain places during different tides. The wading angler needs to know the tide to determine what locations offer safe wading. Safety might not be a factor along open beaches when you plan to only walk the shoreline, but the fishing may be best at times of higher water. At such times, walking out a long distance from shore on flats in a big-tide area requires planning. The tide should be near low so that you can access the flat's edge and reach the fish; but you must know when to leave so you can safely walk back before the flat begins to fill on the incoming tide. Ten-foot tides cover ground quickly. If you must walk a long distance back to shore, leave with enough time to avoid being trapped by the coming water.

The boat angler needs to think about tides for navigation. In locations with heavy structure and big tides, poor planning can get expensive and ruin a fishing trip. Making one mistake can easily cost you the lower unit on your motor. Know where to run safely at all tides, and watch the wind blowing against a strong rip. Outflows that surge into open ocean get ugly when the water begins running out. The wind will pick up a rip, making it even more dangerous to the small boater.

Openings that flow into open water have a lag time; they won't begin to empty immediately after high water. Some outflows feature a delay of several hours or more. This is important for fishing, whether you're wading or boating. Keep records of the different outflows you fish so you can predict when the flow will change. And expect these times to change during different moon phases or when the wind blows from different directions. Full-moon and new-moon tides will be bigger than quarter-moon tides. A full-moon tide is bigger at night; the new moon creates a bigger daytime tide.

THE RIGHT TIDES FOR DIFFERENT PLACES

Beaches, both ocean and sheltered, offer the best opportunities on the last two hours of incoming tides and first two hours of outgoing. I like flats in big-tide areas on the last of the falling tide and the first of the incoming. Flats in small-tide areas seem to have more action during the entire incoming tide. Openings are usually good at the beginnings of both the incoming and outgoing flows. On offshore reefs and rips, the slack and start of each flow are generally the better times to fish, but this differs in many locations. Some places might be good so long as there is moving water, but you need to spend enough time to determine the best tide in different locations. Consult charts for tides in the area you're fishing. The *Eldridge Tide and Pilot Book,* found in most marine supply stores, has comprehensive tide information in each tidal zone from Maine to Florida, and is an invaluable tool for the traveling angler.

JOIN THE CCA

Become a member of your local Coastal Conservation Association. The CCA has become the voice and vehicle of saltwater anglers, fighting to help save our fishery and environment. There are people out there who want to ruin this fishery for their own gain. Don't let it happen. Fight to save something you enjoy. Become a member, be aware of the threats to your fishery, and become active so your voice is heard. Join the CCA.

INDEX